CROSSBILL GUIDES

Lanzarote and Fuerteventura

SPAIN

Crossbill Guides: Lanzarote and Fuerteventura, Spain
First print: 2014
Second, revised print: 2023

Initiative, text and research: Dirk Hilbers, Kees Woutersen, Constant Swinkels
Additional research, text and information: John Cantelo, Kim Lotterman, Albert Vliegenthart, Gino Smeulders
Editing: John Cantelo, Brian Clews, Jack Folkers, Cees Hilbers, Riet Hilbers, Kim Lotterman
Illustrations: Horst Wolter
Maps: Dirk Hilbers, Alex Tabak
Type and image setting: Oscar Lourens
Print: ORO grafic projectmanagement / PNB Letland

ISBN 978-94-91648-26-7

This book is made with FSC-certified paper. The printing process is CO2-neutral through carbon-offsetting. To compensate for the CO2-emissions of the printing processes, we've invested in the project 'Sustainable farming for the future'. For more information, see www.southpole.com under the listed project. You can find the certificate of the carbon-offset on our website under 'downloads' on the Rhodope Mountains Guidebook page.

Published by Crossbill Guides in association with KNNV Publishing.

KNNV Publishing

www.crossbillguides.org
www.knnvpublishing.nl
www.saxifraga.nl

CROSSBILL
GUIDES
FOUNDATION

This guidebook is a product of the non-profit foundation Crossbill Guides. By publishing these books we want to introduce more people to the joys of Europe's beautiful natural heritage and to increase the understanding of the ecological values that underlie conservation efforts. Most of this heritage is protected for ecological reasons and we want to provide insight into these reasons to the public at large. By doing so we hope that more people support the ideas behind nature conservation.
For more information about us and our guides you can visit our website at:

WWW.CROSSBILLGUIDES.ORG

Highlights of Lanzarote and Fuerteventura

1 Witness the results of the gigantic forces that shape the Earth in Lanzarote's spectacular craters, lava fields and massif cliff walls (route 2 and 5).

2 Rise at dawn and track down the desert birds, like Houbara Bustard, Cream-coloured Courser, and the endemic Canary Island Chat (route 3, 8 and 9).

3 See the amazing, colourful, subtropical ocean life by snorkelling or from the comfort of a glass-bottom boat or submarine (page 161).

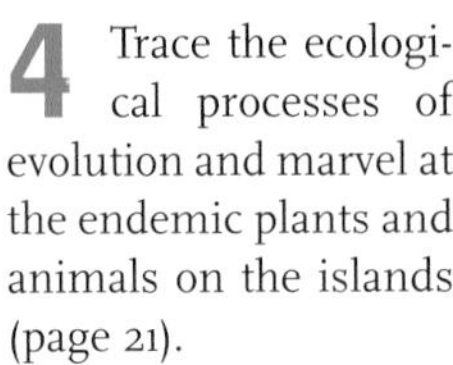

4 Trace the ecological processes of evolution and marvel at the endemic plants and animals on the islands (page 21).

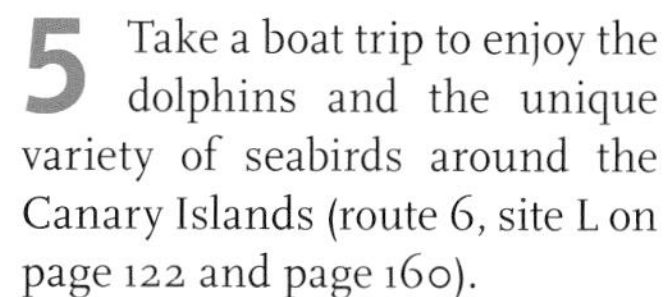

5 Take a boat trip to enjoy the dolphins and the unique variety of seabirds around the Canary Islands (route 6, site L on page 122 and page 160).

6 Hike through the barrancos and along the cliffs and marvel at the rich and sometimes bizarrely shaped flora of these desert islands (route 4, 8, 9, 10 and 11).

7 Island hop to appreciate the different landscapes, flora and fauna.

8 Cycle round La Graciosa and imagine yourself in the landscape of the Canaries before the arrival of Man (route 6).

About this guide

boat trip or ferry crossing

car route

bicycle route

walking route

beautiful scenery

interesting history

interesting geology

This guide is meant for all those who enjoy being in and learning about nature, whether you already know all about it or not. It is set up a little differently from most guides. We focus on explaining the natural and ecological features of an area rather than merely describing the site. We choose this approach because the nature of an area is more interesting, enjoyable and valuable when seen in the context of its complex relationships. The interplay of different species with each other and with their environment is astonishing. The clever tricks and gimmicks that are put to use to beat life's challenges are as fascinating as they are countless.

Take our namesake the Crossbill: at first glance it is just a big finch with an awkward bill. But there is more to the Crossbill than meets the eye. This bill is beautifully adapted for life in coniferous forests. It is used like scissors to cut open pinecones and eat the seeds that are unobtainable for other birds. In the Scandinavian countries where Pine and Spruce take up the greater part of the forests, several Crossbill species have each managed to answer two of life's most pressing questions: how to get food and avoid direct competition. By evolving crossed bills, each differing subtly, they have secured a monopoly of the seeds produced by cones of varying sizes. So complex is this relationship that scientists are still debating exactly how many different species of Crossbill actually exist. Now this should heighten the appreciation of what at first glance was merely a plumb red bird with a beak that doesn't close properly. Once its interrelationships are seen, nature comes alive, wherever you are.

To some, impressed by the 'virtual' familiarity that television has granted to the wilderness of the Amazon, the vastness of the Serengeti or the sublimity of Yellowstone, European nature may seem a puny surrogate, good merely for the casual stroll. In short, the argument seems to be that if you haven't seen a Jaguar, Lion or Grizzly Bear, then you haven't seen the 'real thing'. Nonsense, of course.

But where to go? And how? What is there to see? That is where this guide comes in. We describe the how, the why, the when, the where and the how come of Europe's most beautiful areas. In clear and accessible language, we explain the nature of Lanzarote and Fuerteventura and refer extensively to routes where the area's features can be observed best. We try to make Lanzarote and Fuerteventura come alive. We hope that we succeed.

How to use this guide

This guidebook contains a descriptive and a practical section. The descriptive part comes first and gives you insight into the most striking and interesting natural features of the area. It provides an understanding of what you will see when you go out exploring. The descriptive part consists of a landscape section (marked with a red bar), describing the habitats, the history and the landscape in general, and of a flora and fauna section (marked with a green bar), which discusses the plants and animals that occur in the region.
The second part offers the practical information (marked with a purple bar). A series of routes (walks and car drives) are carefully selected to give you a good flavour of all the habitats, flora and fauna that Lanzarote and Fuerteventura have to offer. At the start of each route description, a number of icons give a quick overview of the characteristics of each route. These icons are explained in the margin of this page. The final part of the book (marked with blue squares) provides some basic tourist information and some tips on finding plants, birds and other animals.
There is no need to read the book from cover to cover. Instead, each small chapter stands on its own and refers to the routes most suitable for viewing the particular features described in it. Conversely, descriptions of each route refer to the chapters that explain more in depth the most typical features that can be seen along the way.
In the back of the guide we have included a list of all the mentioned plant and animal species, with their scientific names and translations into German and Dutch. Some species names have an asterix (*) following them. This indicates that there is no official English name for this species and that we have taken the liberty of coining one. We realise this will meet with some reservations by those who are familiar with scientific names. For the sake of readability however, we have decided to translate the scientific name, or, when this made no sense, we gave a name that best describes the species' appearance or distribution. Please note that we do not want to claim these as the official names. We merely want to make the text easier to follow for those not familiar with scientific names. An overview of the area described in this book is given on the map on page 13. For your convenience we have also turned the inner side of the back flap into a map of the area indicating all the described routes. Descriptions in the explanatory text refer to these routes.

interesting flora

interesting invertebrate life

interesting reptile and amphibian life

interesting mammals

interesting birdlife

site for snorkelling

interesting for whales and dolphins

visualising the ecological contexts described in this guide

Table of contents

List of text boxes

LANDSCAPE

According to one European airline's adverts, the sole reason for coming to Lanzarote and Fuerteventura is their beautiful beaches. With this claim they summarise the image most people have of these islands. They couldn't be more wrong!

Lanzarote and Fuerteventura are isolated, semi-desert islands off the coast of North-Africa. They are also known as the Eastern Canary Islands, and lie somewhat apart from their neighbours, the western Canaries (Gran Canaria, Tenerife, La Gomera, La Palma and El Hierro). Lanzarote and Fuerteventura share with the other islands the wonderful flora and fauna that is so unique to the Canary archipelago but add to that some traits of the African Sahara. A visit to Lanzarote and Fuerteventura (it is easy to visit both in a single trip) is a journey to stunning isolated desert landscapes, the world of volcanoes, and an exploration to the very birth and evolution of life with unique, endemic plant and animal species. And yes, time permitting, you can visit one of those beautiful beaches as well.

The islands' reputations as a sun, surf and overwintering destination developed as late as the 1990s. In their wake, courtesy of frequent, inexpensive charter flights, the islands were discovered by birders and naturalists. The big draw at first were the endemic and hard-to-find-elsewhere desert birds, but soon an appreciation grew for the photogenic landscapes, the volcanism, and the unique habitats, which are intrinsically linked to oceanic islands (as our book will show). Landscapes range from rocky shores, coastal sand dunes and arid semi-desert plains to rocky black lava flows. Groups of palm trees, cliffs and ravines and even the tourist resorts add to an exotic feel for European visitors.

This book will help you to discover the birds, the flora, the landscape and all the interesting features of Lanzarote and Fuerteventura.

The rolling red hills of Betancuria, Fuerteventura.

Geographical overview

The area described in this book comprises Fuerteventura, Lanzarote and several small islands nearby. Together, these are the Eastern Canary Islands, situated about 100 kms off the South Moroccan coast. They belong to the Spanish province of Las Palmas (which also comprises Gran Canaria) that is again part of the autonomous region of Las Islas Canarias. The northern island Lanzarote (size approx. 850 km^2) is situated just a little over 10 km from Fuerteventura (size approx. 1660 km^2) to the south. The distance to the nearest of the western Canary Islands, Gran Canaria, is nearly 100 kms, almost as far as the African coast. Hence, Lanzarote and Fuerteventura are quite isolated from the other Canary Islands. In terms of nature, they reflect their geographic position quite well, as they have both strong Canarian and Saharan characteristics.

Lanzarote

The capital of Lanzarote is Arrecife, which has about 61,000 inhabitants and is situated on the east coast of the island. The other larger towns all lie on the southeast coast. In the west lies Timanfaya National Park (route 2), which consists of a huge expanse of bare lava created during major volcanic outbursts between 1730 and 1739. North of Timanfaya you find the desert plain of Teguise (route 3), which is the best area for desert birds on the island. A little further north, rise the majestic Famara cliffs (route 4), which form the botanical hotspot of Lanzarote. Here, at 671 metres, is Lanzarote's highest peak, Peñas del Chache, which is recognisable from far away thanks to two enormous radar domes for air traffic control.
From Lanzarote's northernmost village of Órzola, you can take the ferry to the island of La Graciosa, which is the largest and only inhabited island of the Chinijo archipelago (route 6).

Fuerteventura

Puerto del Rosario is the capital of Fuerteventura and has about 39,000 inhabitants. The total population of Fuerteventura is smaller than that of Lanzarote, but the island is about twice as big. Like Lanzarote, Fuerteventura consists of desert plains and desert mountains. The largest plains are in the north, near La Oliva (route 8), and in the centre, near Antigua (site C on page 147). Arid mountains dominate the landscape in Betancuria (routes 10 and 11), in the Cuchillos de Vigán (site G on page 149) and in the far south, on the peninsula de la Jandía (route 12). Here lies the highest peak of Fuerteventura: the Pico de la Zarza (812 m; route 13).

La Jandía is connected to the rest of Fuerteventura by the isthmus of sandy desert of Costa Calma (route 12 and site I on page 150).
Fuerteventura and Lanzarote are connected by two car ferry services – one between the two capitals, and another much shorter service that crosses the narrow strait between both islands, connecting Playa Blanca (Lanzarote) with Corralejo (Fuerteventura).
Both Lanzarote and Fuerteventura are essentially desert islands, though they differ in a few important details. Lanzarote is popularly known as 'the island of volcanoes' and has indeed a more pronounced volcanic landscape than Fuerteventura. The latter is the island of the vast expanses

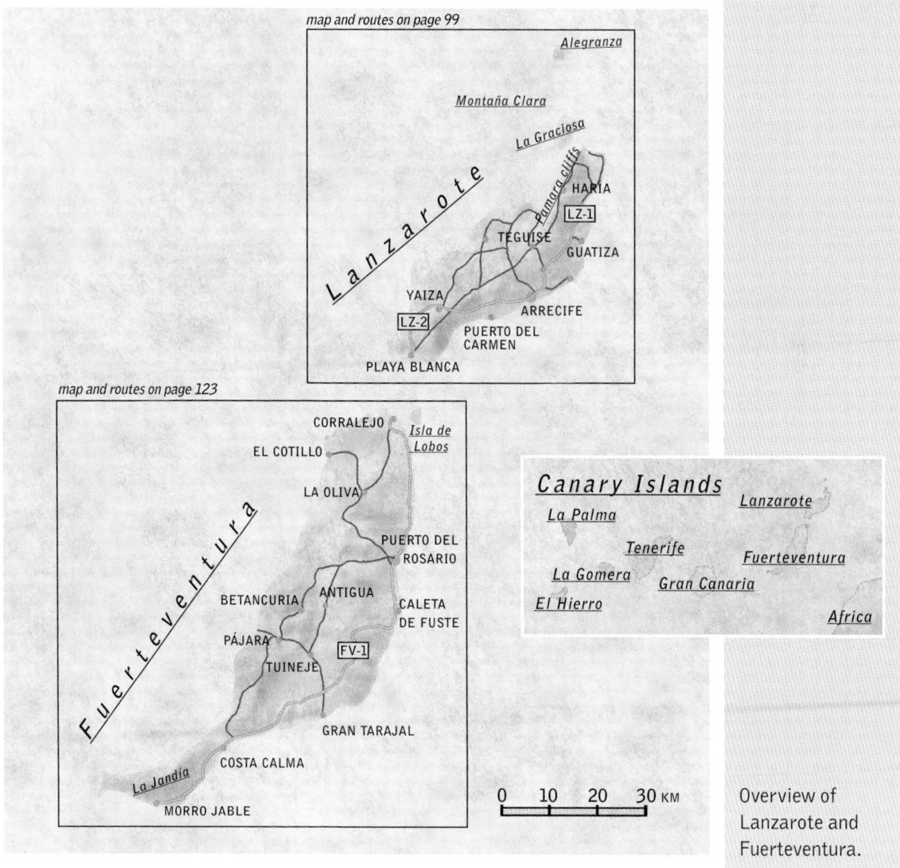

Overview of Lanzarote and Fuerteventura.

The slopes covered with volcanic gravel or lapilli form a surreal landscape. This landscape is at its most impressive in Timanfaya National Park (route 2).

of windy desert plains, although on a smaller scale, these are present on Lanzarote as well.

All of the five major landscape types (desert plains, ravines or barrancos, sandy and rocky coasts and human-made environments) are present on both islands, but the extent to which they are present differs. There are more desert plains on Fuerteventura and they are more frequently sandy or stony in character, while those on Lanzarote consist predominantly of lapilli (black volcanic gravel) and of lava fields. Both islands have cliffs, but those on Lanzarote have a richer vegetation and a different set of breeding birds, which include Barbary Falcon, Eleonora's Falcon, Osprey and a number of sea birds absent from Fuerteventura. That island's trump card is the endemic Fuerteventura Stonechat, but it also supports much larger numbers of Trumpeter Finch and Egyptian Vulture.

Although most naturalists seem to prefer Fuerteventura over Lanzarote, in our opinion you really need to visit both islands. And why not? The boat only takes 25 minutes.

Macaronesia and the Canary Islands – a different world

Biologically the Canary Islands are not a part of Europe, but of Macaronesia – a somewhat obscure name for the well-known archipelagos of the Azores, Madeira, Selvages, the Cape Verde Islands and the Canaries. All of them are volcanic islands, situated in the Atlantic off the coasts of Europe and Africa. They are biologically different from the nearby continents because of their isolation, both currently and historically, as there never was a land bridge linking them to the mainland. However, the Macaronesian islands, despite being isolated from one another, do share some biological characteristics since they are climatically quite similar. All of them exhibit a type of subtropical climate that, although now only present here, was, in Tertiary times (before the ice ages), widespread in Europe and North-Africa. Hence the Macaronesian Islands form their own biological world, sharing between them many closely related species, some of which are relicts of ones that were widespread on the continents in Tertiary times.

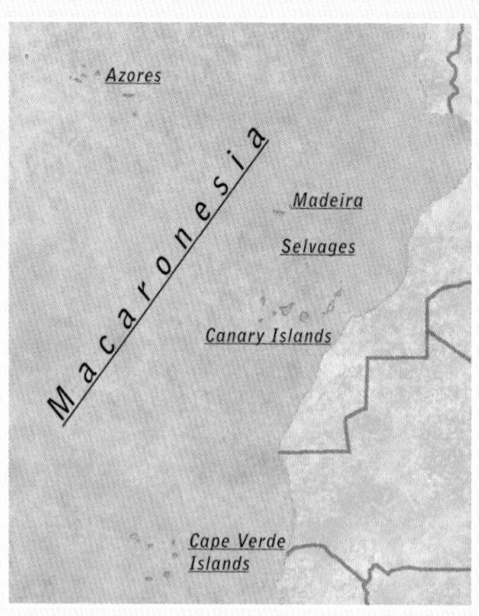

The Canary Islands and Madeira are at the heart of this Macaronesian ecoregion. The Western Canary Islands (El Hierro, La Palma, La Gomera, Tenerife and Gran Canaria) all share an extremely rugged terrain, with lushly vegetated north slopes and dry south facing slopes typified by succulent plants with thick, water-storing stems and leaves. Lanzarote and Fuerteventura lie much closer to Africa than the other islands and are much flatter and desert-like.

The Canary islands

	Surface km²	Perimeter km.	Max. Altitude m.	Population (2019)
El Hierro	269	110	1,501	11,154
La Palma	708	166	2,423	84,793
La Gomera	370	100	1,487	22,100
Tenerife	2.034	342	3,718	949,471
Gran Canaria	1.560	256	1,949	865,756
Fuerteventura	1.660	304	807	122,629
Lanzarote incl. La Graciosa	846	191	671	150,998

Geology

Lanzarote exhibits perhaps the widest range of volcanic features of all the Canary Islands. Recent lava fields and extremely hot lava surfaces can be seen in Timanfaya National Park (route 2). Route 5 and site D visit another crater. Route 2, 5 and site H visit recent lava fields. The Famara cliffs (route 3 and 4 and site J) are a strong example of erosion.
On Fuerteventura, craters and lava fields are part of route 8 and of sites A, B and G. Areas overblown with marine sand feature on routes 8 and 12 as well as on sites B and I.

The world's islands all fall into two distinct categories: those that were once part of a bigger land mass and those that have always been isolated by the sea. From a biological point of view, these two types of islands are fundamentally different. The first type started out with a biological heritage – the flora and fauna of the mainland to which it was once attached. The second has always been isolated and started as a biological tabula rasa (see page 21).

The Canaries belong to the second type of island. In origin, they are akin to the islands of Hawaii, Iceland and the Galapagos. In contrast, all the Mediterranean islands and the British Isles are examples of islands that were once connected to the larger land masses of Europe or Africa.

The geological origin of the Canary Islands and of the other Oceanic islands mentioned above is volcanic. Volcanic eruptions brought magma up to the surface, which built up until it rose out of the ocean.

Although there is still some controversy about the exact geological origin of the Canary volcanoes, the usual theory is that the islands are formed on so-called hotspots. These are places with very high volcanic activity, because an unusually thin earth crust covers the underlying magma mantle. The hotspot that gave rise to the Canary Islands is in the contact zone where the thick continental crust meets a much thinner oceanic one. Magma was pushed up periodically from a sea floor about 4,000 metres below. The first volcanic activity took place here about 60 million years ago and the most recent one was in 2021 on La Palma!

Lanzarote and Fuerteventura are, with ages of about 20 million years, the oldest of the Canary Islands. They are part of a single volcanic eruption platform that gradually drifted eastwards with the tectonic movement of the oceanic plate, until new eruptions gave rise to the next island – Gran Canaria. Then followed Tenerife, La Gomera, La Palma, and finally El Hierro, which is a geological infant of only 1.1 million years old.

Opposite page: The geological birth of Lanzarote and Fuerteventura took place 20 million years ago from volcanic eruptions from a mantle plume – a thin spot in the earth's crust. As the tectonic movements caused hotspot to move further east, new islands arose from subsequent eruptions from the mantle plume, while remnant magma chambers kept volcanism alive on Lanzarote and Fuerteventura. Currently, the island of El Hierro lies right above the hotspot.

Volcanic activity did not stop as islands drifted away from the hotspot zone. Eruptions have taken place on all the islands (except on La Gomera) during the last million years, while on Lanzarote, Tenerife, La Palma and El Hierro major eruptions have taken place in the past five centuries). The one on Lanzarote gave rise to the Malpaís of Timanfaya (route 2), and lasted 5 years, 7 months and 16 days (see box on page 20).

The geological evolution of an island

Eruptions are usually thought of as a singular, spectacular event in which a big, cone-shaped mountain rises up, violently gushing out fountains of red-hot lava that subsequently bury everything in its path under a thick soup of flaming liquid rock. This is, indeed, one way an eruption can take place. Of all possible forms of eruptions, this one is at the extreme violent end of the spectrum.

Broadly speaking, there are two types of eruptions. Magma can ooze out quietly from one or several points, or it can appear suddenly. In either case, there is usually more than one eruption. These may occur in varying intervals. In fact, these intervals are so irregular, that it can be difficult to say when an eruption ends and a volcano becomes dormant. When Timanfaya erupted for over five years, the lava did not flow the entire time. Considering the 2021 eruption on La Palma, it might well be possible that another eruption could happen next year or the one after that.

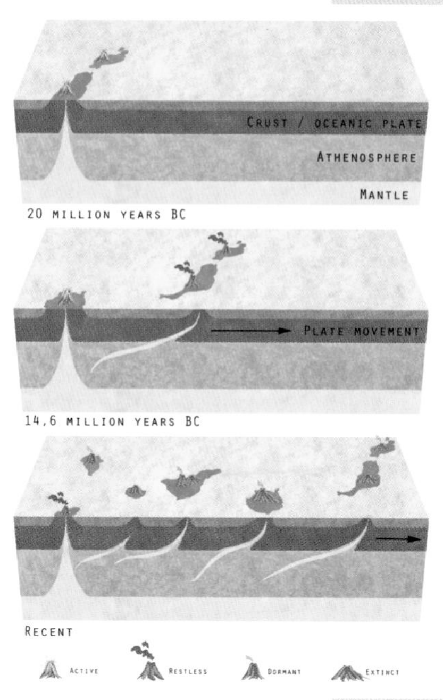

Depending on how the lava solidified and its chemical composition, the volcanic rocks of Lanzarote and Fuerteventura take on a variety of shapes. The bedrock is usually composed of basalts or trachytes (or a mixture of the two). The essential difference between them is the amount of silica, which is the most abundant component in magma. Basalts, which have a lower silica content, are darker and basic or alkaline while trachytes, with their higher silica content, are paler and acidic. After their emergence and rapid growth,

Lanzarote and Fuerteventura entered a long phase of erosion. In the early stages, the islands must have looked like El Hierro and Tenerife: high and with steep slopes and deep gorges. In spite of small, relatively recent eruptions (including the Timanfaya eruptions of the 18th century) erosion and sedimentation has gradually reshaped the islands. Debris filled the ravines and valleys, creating plains, flattening tops and smoothing the edges. Gradually the landscape was remodelled. The process was aided by the fierce winds that brought in marine sand that filled in the lowlands. These sands are predominantly of organic origin – crushed and pulverised seashells washed ashore together with eroded volcanic material were blown further inland. Sahara sand is also blown over from the mainland to the islands, but takes up a smaller portion of the sandy deserts of Fuerteventura and Lanzarote.

The result is the smoothened topography of Fuerteventura and Lanzarote we find today – much smoother in any case than the rugged young islands you find in the west of the archipelago. The striking exceptions are the huge cliffs of La Jandía (Fuerteventura) and Famara (Lanzarote). These are the result of erosion as well, but this time it is the perpetual undermining effect of the waves that created the landscape. The sea 'eats away' the land, leaving high cliffs as a result.

The geology of both islands is quite similar, but there are a few differences as well. Fuerteventura has a proportionally larger area of sedimentary soils – mainly sands. It also has strongly eroded, sharp mountain ridges known locally as *cuchillos* (knives).

Lanzarote has more traces of recent volcanic activity. There are many craters, all over the central part of the island. The vast area covered by lava fields is an exquisite example of recent volcanism. These fields are very rough, like a grotesque magnification of ploughed land, but with hard, sharp lumps of lava. It is useless for agriculture (or anything else), hence the Spanish name of *malpaís* – bad land.

Climate

The climate on Lanzarote and Fuerteventura is pleasant throughout the year. It is not as mild as on the western islands, but surely much friendlier than the nearby African mainland. There are two factors that determine the benign climate: the trade winds and the ocean's Canary Current. The even temperature, with little variation between seasons and even between day and night, is very typical. This is a result of the constant temperature of the ocean. During the winter months, temperatures vary between a pleasant 21 °C at midday and 15 °C at night. Sheltered from the wind, but

in the sun, the midday temperatures can feel much higher. In the evening, it is often warm enough to sit outside. This is why these islands are such attractive winter holiday destinations.
In the summer, the thermometer hovers between 32 °C during the day and 20 °C at night. Rain is scarce, because, in contrast to the western islands, there are no mountain barriers to push the moist air upwards to cool and fall as rain. The average annual rainfall is about 140 mm – typical for semi-deserts. In comparison, Amsterdam receives on average 800 mm per year and London 600 mm.
Rain falls between October and late March, but even in this period there are only 16 days on average with precipitation. The southern parts of Lanzarote and Fuerteventura enjoy as many as 2,500 hours of sunshine annually.
The wind is almost a permanent factor on both islands (one interpretation of the name Fuerteventura is 'strong wind'). The prevailing winds come from the northeast, but occasionally, a scorching hot and dry sandstorm known as la Calima blows in from the Sahara Desert (similar to the Sirocco wind that blows Saharan sand across Europe). The fierce wind brings in fine white sand, and even large insects like locusts to the island. These hot-spells usually last for no more than a few days. The north of Lanzarote is usually windier, cloudier and a little wetter due to the

The bizarrely shaped volcanic malpaís (right) forms the youngest bedrock on the islands. The eroded plains, covered in with sand, are much older (left).

Timanfaya, the fire mountain

The Timanfaya lava fields on Lanzarote are part of the Timanfaya National Park which covers about a fourth of the island. The eruptions in the 18th century have given us some of the most important accounts of volcanism in modern times. It was a spectacular event that continued, with intervals, for more than five years. This was witnessed by a local priest who lived a few kilometres away, in the village of Yaiza. That he survived is a miracle, considering the fact that life on much of the island was extinguished. His written account states:

"The first day of September, 1730, between nine and ten at night, the earth suddenly opened near Timanfaya, two leagues of Yaiza. On the first night an enormous mountain rose up from the earth, and flames came out of the peak which kept burning for nineteen days".

The land that was buried under the lava was some of the most fertile of the island, where grain and vegetables were cultivated. A total of 20 (!) villages were buried and 420 buildings were destroyed. All crops were lost, farm animals died, the wells vaporised and farmland was buried forever. Many people died, either directly or as a result of toxic fumes, and those who survived were left without property or the means for survival.

And today, all this is a National Park. Think about that fertile land when you visit this otherworldly, Mars-like landscape.

Because the eruptions were so relatively recent (the last one was in 1824), you can see some of the more spectacular features of volcanism. In one area that is often visited on guided excursions (part of route 2), the temperature just 10 metres below the surface is 600 ° C. Only 10 centimetres under the plastic soles of your neighbour's flipflops (surely you thought of putting on proper footwear!), the temperature is as high as 160° C.

During strong easterlies, sand is blown over the islands and deposited on the plains. Corralejo Nature Park, Fuerteventura.

moist trade winds. Because the cliffs form the highest point on the island, rising straight out of the sea, they are basically the first thing the wind meets when it hits Lanzarote. The trade winds are especially frequent in summer, just when they are needed to cool down the atmosphere and are nearly constant in the month of July. Equally, the massive cliffs of La Jandía and the mountains of Betancuria on Fuerteventura purge a bit more water from the air.

Evolution

Life on Lanzarote and Fuerteventura is easy. Tourists come to take some time off from the complexities of everyday life. In a way, nature has done the same. Lanzarote and Fuerteventura rose from the sea as a biologically blank sheet of paper without a living thing on it. Hence nature's routines and ways had to be re-written. This is why islands like Fuerteventura and Lanzarote – in fact all Canary Islands – are such exciting places for biologists.

It is on isolated oceanic islands like these that that the processes of evolution and the formation of ecosystems are best witnessed. Their start can be traced back to just a few events of colonisation. These islands are giant outdoor laboratories of evolution, with the odd, endemic life forms being their products.

It is not at all difficult to plan your visit with the aim of understanding the evolution of life and the establishment of ecosystems. It's certainly a lot cheaper and closer than joining most 'evolution tourists' on the Galapagos Islands! In fact, it gives you a fascinating, spectacular and beautiful insight into nature, but, as you'll see further on, it also grants us a frightening window into a possible future.

We have designed this chapter as an armchair excursion through some of the places on Lanzarote and Fuerteventura that form the narrative of the process of evolution.

Stop 1: How it all began – Timanfaya, Lanzarote

Truly clean slates in evolutionary terms are rare in the world, but in Timanfaya National Park on Lazarote, you have an example (route 2). Large parts consist of lava spat out less than 300 years ago. This is the hottest and most recent volcanic ground on Lanzarote and is pretty much devoid of life. Only one group of organisms has already been able to colonise this barren ground: lichens.

At its most basic form, life needs two elements: building blocks for a body (water, carbon, nitrogen and several other elements) and energy to make and maintain such a body. On Timanfaya, these requirements are hard to come by. Lichens are super organisms – an alliance between algae and fungi. These two very different life forms are so tightly woven together that we can actually talk of lichen species. The algal component of the lichen is, like most plants, able to use the sun's energy to take up carbon, while the fungal part is able to absorb minerals from rock. Hence lichens can survive almost anywhere on earth, even here on the 'Fire Mountain'.

Stop 2: the islotes of Timanfaya – Lanzarote

Driving through Timanfaya, you'll eventually come to a place where the monotony of the lichen-clad lavas is interrupted by a vegetated spot. The Spanish call it an islote, an islet of old lava that wasn't covered by the 18th century eruptions.

Here odd-looking, thick-stemmed bushes cover the slopes – bushes of a kind you won't find outside the Canary Islands. Most common are Balsam Spurge and King Juba's Spurge, members of a family with a worldwide distribution, but these particular (sub)species occur only on the Canaries. The seeds of these plants are far too heavy for the wind to carry them, and the occurrence of such species on volcanic islands is one of these key pieces in the evolutionary puzzle. The seeds of such plants are likely to have travelled as cargo in the bellies of birds, such as pigeons, that strayed too far from the coast and found the inhospitable bare islands as their only place to land. A lucky poop on a bit of soil (thanks to the lichen cover there is now some soil and not just bare rock) and the colonisation of the island is thus underway.

There are other ways of reaching an oceanic island. The most obvious is active flight as exemplified by birds, bats and some insects. Wingless animals sometimes travel

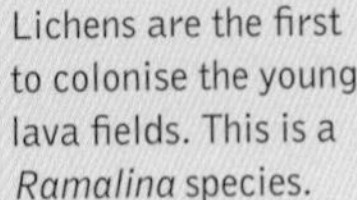

Lichens are the first to colonise the young lava fields. This is a *Ramalina* species.

on 'rafts' of floating plant material. Probably this is how some beetles and other insects arrived along with small lizards and mammals. This is difficult for larger animals hence, on Lanzarote and Fuerteventura we find only one native lizard, skink, gecko and land mammal (a small shrew). This is a considerably less diverse range than seen in non-flying smaller animals like insects. Perversely, many wingless animals currently found on the islands (the beetles are a good example), only lost their capacity for flight once they colonised the islands.
Finally, some animals and plants have exploited mankind's capacity of crossing the oceans. They hitched across on a boat.

Stop 3: the cliffs of La Jandía – Fuerteventura

Now let's travel to the southern tip of Fuerteventura, to the peninsula of La Jandía, where you'll find more plants than just the Balsam Spurge. Alongside it grows the conspicuous, cactus-like Canary Spurge, and the even more prickly Jandía Spurge* (*Euphorbia handiensis*). The latter is, as the name implies, restricted to the very slope on which you stand. It is an endemic, occurring nowhere else in the world.
The odd thing about the flora of La Jandía (and much of the Canaries) is the presence of many endemic species, which mostly belong to just a few plant families. On the Canaries, the spurges (*Euphorbia*), buglosses (*Echium*), houseleeks (*Aeonium, Aichryson*) and the daisy family (*Asteraceae*) are well represented. One very special daisy, the Winter's Marguerite* (*Argyranthemum winteri*), is also found exclusively on these slopes.
This odd botanical composition (very few families with many endemic species) is typical of volcanic islands and is due to two different processes each enhancing the other. First, colonisations are few. The land birds that stray this far out from land tend to be migrants so are unlikely to stay to breed whilst rafts of plants that accidentally wash up these shores are still fewer. Consequently, those lucky plants that did manage to establish themselves, had the whole islands pretty much for themselves. They could quickly spread, making it more difficult for new arrivals to find their own niche. This explains why there are very few species groups.
Secondly, each new arrival on an island brings with it a very small range of genes, just those of the few specimens that managed to establish themselves. Rarely are these a good representation of the vast gene pool of the mainland population. The majority of the unusual and some of the characteristic genetic traits will be lacking, whereas others that were rare in the original population will be over-represented. These rare

traits will suddenly become common in the new population, and within a few generations, the genetic make-up of the island population will be very different from that of the mainland – a process called genetic drift. Reproduction in isolation with an odd subset of genes is the fastest way for a new species to evolve.

Succulent scrub consisting of King Juba's Spurge, Balsam Spurge and Verode. The spurge family shows an exceptional diversity of species on the Canary Islands, begging the evolutionary question: why so many species, belonging to so few families?

Stop 4: the cliffs of Famara – Lanzarote

On Lanzarote there are steep slopes too. The Famara cliffs (route 4) are not unlike those of La Jandía: spectacular, north-facing cliffs at the edge of the ocean. Here you find another marguerite – a pretty yellow one this time, called Madeira's Marguerite (*Argyranthemum maderense*), which is, confusingly, an endemic wildflower of Lanzarote. If you were to visit Gran Canaria, Tenerife, or the other islands, you could add many more marguerites to the list.

On our previous stop at La Jandía it became clear why only few species groups are on the islands and why they are represented by endemic species, but how is it possible that there are so many different endemic species within that same group? Why four instead of a single spurge? Three instead of one houseleek?

The Canary Marguerites are well studied and are like the botanical version of Darwin's Finches. There are 24 species in total, of which 20 are endemic to the Canary Islands with the others found only on the other Macaronesian islands. They are a textbook example of how speciation on islands takes place. The first 'proto-Marguerite' seed germinated on

Fuerteventura, arriving from Africa via a passing bird. As it flourished, the species' genetic make-up quickly changed from the ancestral species through genetic drift. Later, due to another chance event, a little seed from the Fuerteventuran population arrived on Lanzarote. Yet another period of genetic drift split the Lanzarote Marguerite from the Fuerteventura one. And then a seed arrived on Gran Canaria etc. To each island its own Marguerite.

Meanwhile there is also a process of adaptation taking place. The new environmental conditions favour a genetic makeup that provides the best adaptations to novel conditions. Here the plant's genetic imprint will soon 'drift' towards the characteristics needed to survive in these different conditions – that is, if these genes are present in the original population, or if mutations allowed these traits to develop. This is the process Darwin described as being key to evolution: natural selection. It explains why succulence has become such a dominant trait of Canary Island plants: it is the perfect adaptation to survive here. It is also why Tenerife, which has a much more varied set of ecosystems, is home to nine species of Marguerite, each adapted to its own habitat. Fuerteventura, ecologically a much less diverse island, has only one.

So isolated islands with a variety of habitats and limited genetic input are true biodiversity generators. It is here that the motors of evolution go full throttle, creating many different species from a narrow genetic base coming from only a few families of plants.

Shrubby Marguarite, the most common and widespread of the 24 species of Marguarites on the Canary islands. All except 4 are endemic to the archipelago.

Stop 5: the desert

Enough about plants. What about birds? Very early in the morning, the central desert plains of Lanzarote (route 3) give you a good opportunity to get to grips with the birds of the island. With good light and decent optics, it isn't hard to notice that most bird species are a little different from their mainland relatives. The Buzzard is slightly lighter in colour and more streaked below. The Kestrel is darker and males have a darker grey head. Indeed, for resident island birds distinct subspecies are almost the norm. There are island races of Egyptian Vulture, Houbara Bustard, Trumpeter Finch, Raven and Great Grey Shrike (see also box on page 78). Clearly, it is

The Canarian Ravens are not (yet) considered separate species, but merely as a subspecies. However, it is clearly different from its European relative, being much smaller and having a brown neck and a different call.

not only the plants with so many endemics on the Canaries. Bird populations are also changing and evolving in new forms.
But there is a big difference between birds and plants. A viable bird population needs much more space.

Stop 6: La Graciosa

The small islet of La Graciosa is clearly visible from the miradores on the Famara cliffs (route 4). The ferry crosses the small strait between Lanzarote and La Graciosa in less than half an hour (route 6). Walking along the wave beaten coastal rocks of this small island, you may enjoy a small flight of Turnstones, and perhaps Whimbrel. Nevertheless, it is oddly silent, because there is one vital element missing: the Canary Islands or Black Oystercatcher (see page 86-87). This bird sadly became extinct sometime in the 20th century. Why is uncertain, but there are plenty of theories! A little further inland, there is a similar emptiness as the local subspecies of the Fuerteventura Stonechat is no more. Reason unknown.
Here, we come to the question of extinction. Why do some species disappear while others flourish? Small islands can only support small populations. Since natural populations always fluctuate, it takes only a little to bring a population to the brink of extinction. Add a disaster, such as the Timanfaya eruption, and the extinction often follows.

La Graciosa – once home to the endemic Black Oystercatcher and the Chinijo Stonechat. Both are now extinct (see page 86-87).

Stop 7: Betancuria mountains

Populations on small islands are also vulnerable, because many species evolved under conditions where there were only a limited number of threats. Developing in isolation, without even small terrestrial animals, island ecosystems are vulnerable to alien intruders. Sources of food, be they animal or vegetable, have not developed protective defences. Any introduction, intended or accidental, can then be a true 'game changer', wiping out existing species in mere generations. Such introductions are human induced. We brought large herbivores (goats) to the islands, which roam freely and favour the slightly greener locations, such as the Betancuria mountains. And we brought cats and rats. And these changed the appearance of the Canaries forever.

The cause of many ecological problems on Fuerteventura: the goats that strip the island of its vegetation.

On a global scale, islands suffer the biggest loss of species. The list of Canary Island extinctions, human induced or otherwise, is long and contains the likes of the Giant Rat, the Lava Mouse, the Giant Lizard and two shearwaters endemic to Lanzarote and Fuerteventura, to name but a few.

History teaches us that the arrival of people on an oceanic island has a major negative impact on the endemic flora and fauna. On the Canaries this already started with the arrival of the first settlers, the Guanches (see history section). Today we witness the second wave of extinction, that started with the arrival of Europeans on the islands, and still has not reached its climax.

So small, isolated populations can both herald the birth of new species and the demise of an existing one. There is much discussion about the lessons we should learn from island ecology. One of the greatest threats worldwide to nature today is the chopping up of large areas of pristine habitat into smaller pieces. We turn biological continents into a collection of isolated islands – islands with remnant populations of species that require large areas to survive. If the lessons of island ecology are true, they offer a frightening look into a grim future, in which once common plants and animals will grow steadily rarer and slip into extinction simply because their populations become too small. It turns out that life on Lanzarote and Fuerteventura is not as light and easy as it seemed.

Habitats

Descriptions of the Canary Islands are often based on the western islands, which are famous for having two very different landscapes. The south-facing mountain slopes are very hot, dry and desert-like, but northern ones are cloaked in dense, wet cloud forests. The presence of two such extremes in a very small area is striking, beautiful, and seen in only a few places on the planet.

The north-easterly tradewinds are responsible for this sharp contrast in landscape: the moist air that is blown inland from the sea condenses as it is forced up the mountain. Once on the far side, it has lost most of its moisture. When the air drops again to the warm lowland the clouds evaporate.

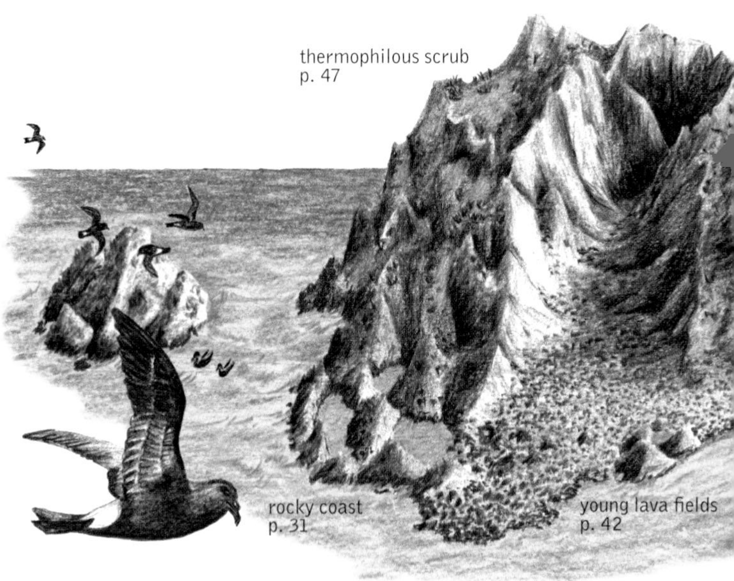

Cross section of an Eastern Canary Island showing the different habitats from north (left) to south (right).

Lanzarote and Fuerteventura lack this near daily process of cloud-formation, because their mountains are not high enough. Only the great cliffs of Famara (Lanzarote) and La Jandía (Fuerteventura) rise to a height sufficient, just, to capture a little humidity. Hence Lanzarote and Fuerteventura largely lack the diversity of Canarian nature. Only on these steep cliffs and hillsides will you find the odd vegetation for which the western islands are famous.

But what Lanzarote and Fuerteventura lack in diversity, they make up for in quality! It is here that you will find a very wide range of arid landscapes, such as stony arid plains, young lava fields and dunes of marine sand. In contrast to the precipitous western islands, there are many rolling desert plains on Lanzarote and Fuerteventura. These level areas are home to a flora and fauna that is either very rare or absent from the Western islands. In particular, the birdlife of these desert plains is rich and attractive.

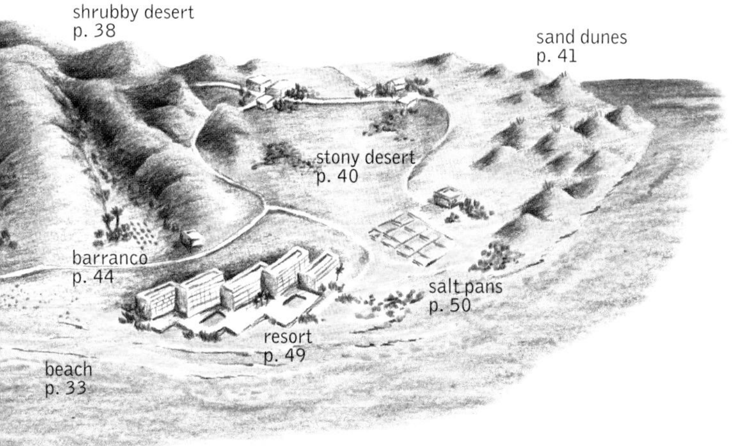

The coast

On Lanzarote, beaches and saltmarshes feature prominently on routes 1, 3 and 6. Tidal pools and rocky coastline are found on route 5 and sites E and H. Marine life is best enjoyed snorkelling at Playa Papagayo (site C) or at the aquarium (site J on page 122). For seabird watching, route 6 is the best. Also look at sites A, B and K.

On Fuerteventura, beaches, tidal pools and lagunas are an element of route 7, 8 and 12. Marine life is best enjoyed at Los Lobos (route 7), but there are also good beaches for snorkelling between Tarajalejo and Costa Calma. To enjoy the sea life of the sub-littoral zone (down 5 to 30 metres deep) you'll have to book a trip with a glass-bottom boat or submarine (see page 157).

The brochures are right about one thing: the most pleasant place to be on these hot and dry islands is the coast, where the sea breeze is refreshing, and the cool sea water so inviting. Fortunately, the coast is also one of the most attractive wildlife habitats. The landscape is stunning, the birdlife is rich, Atlantic Lizards are everywhere, and in winter and spring, there are plenty of special wildflowers. On top of that, the coastal submarine life is superb. Put on your goggles, stick your head in a tidal pool and you

The beautiful pristine sandy coast of La Graciosa (route 6).

The skerries of the lava coast have many tidal pools where sea life and waders are at home.

are eyeball to eyeball with a world that literally makes everything you see in the terrestrial habitats seem pale.
There are two types of coastline on both Lanzarote and Fuerteventura: rocky and sandy.

Rocky coastlines

Much of the coastline of Lanzarote and Fuerteventura is rocky. Black chunks of lava break the ocean's waves. In a strong gale, this offers a spectacular show of crashing waves and foamy fountains of spume. Caught by the wind the watery froth is blown out over the cliffs and rocks.
This is the intertidal zone of the rocky shores. The ecological drivers of this habitat are air and sea water, which play a game of cat and mouse. During high tides and strong onshore winds, the sea is in charge. All the rocky crannies, cracks and pools are deluged with water, and salt spray reaches far inland or stretch high up the cliffs. But at low tide and with little wind, the sea is driven back and evaporation by air and sun erase the water's influence, leaving only the salt behind.
As the tide retreats, fish are trapped in tidal pools and small water holes in the rocks. There are marine species that have well adapted to these conditions. Some crabs and fish can survive this cyclic catch and release

The Whimbrel is one of the most common waders on the rocky coasts of Lanzarote and Fuerteventura.

game. Algae and small limpets attach themselves to the rocks and are able to endure the periods of exposure to sun and air.

For birds, the rocks and tidal pools of the intertidal zone are an excellent place to find food. The major western migration flyway between tropical Africa and Europe passes the West African coast, which is just near enough to Lanzarote and Fuerteventura to draw in part of this huge stream of birds. Pretty much any of the species that travel up and down this flyway, may turn up on the islands' coasts and the tidal pools and rocky shores is where many of them (especially waders) find food and rest to regain their strength. A variety of species, most of which you'd associate with flat expanses of mud, can be found here between the rocks: Common Sandpiper, Dunlin, Ringed and Grey Plovers, Black-tailed and Bar-tailed Godwits, Little Egrets... when the sea is calm, they all rest on the lava outcrops near the sea.

As a habitat for breeding birds, the rocky coast is rather poor. Yellow-legged Gull is perhaps the most typical bird of the coast. Berthelot's Pipit is another bird that is well at home here, but then again, it is frequent all over the islands. Big sea bird colonies as you find in the northern Atlantic are strikingly absent – the rock cliffs are empty. Or they appear to be so, because Lanzarote and Fuerteventura are hugely important islands for sea birds. The species that occur here breed very locally in inaccessible places, mostly on islets off the coast of the main island (see page 84).

Botanically, the rocky coast is a poor habitat. The combination of salt-water spray, extremely low precipitation and porous soils create extreme conditions in which only few plants survive. Interestingly, the physical adaptations needed to survive in saline conditions are similar to that for surviving in drought. Therefore, the succulent growth form, with thick, water-storing leaves and stems that is found in the original semi-desert vegetation, reappears on the rocky coast that is influenced by salt spray (sea water droplets blown in by strong gales).

The flora that has evolved to cope with this situation has some very peculiar species. Especially the Zygophyllum, with its thick and bright green stems and leaves, is a typical sight. Move a little further inland, and soon you will encounter a score of other plants, such as Bassia, Saltwort and Balsam Spurge (see flora chapter for more detail).

Beaches and salt marsh

The white sandy beaches would be just as attractive to migrating birds as the rocky shores, if it weren't for the fact that they are so busy with tourists. Sunworshippers and (worse!) surfers of all sorts have left most beaches too disturbed to attract birds.

Hence, the best beaches (from a naturalist's perspective) are those with large sand banks off the coast (see route 12). These are still frequently used by birds, such as Sandwich Tern, Yellow-legged Gull and a variety of waders.

There are white-sandy beaches and black-sandy beaches. The white sand comes largely from the

Zygophyllum (top) and Traganum (bottom) – the most typical salt tolerant plants of the rocky and sandy coasts respectively.

The threatened Fuerteventura Limpet

Limpets (*Lapas* in Spanish) are an important source of food for birds, fish and people. Their high commercial value has made them an important marine resource in the islands' economies. It has even been suggested that overcollection was instrumental in the extinction of Canary Islands Oystercatcher (see page 86). Limpets have been cooked and eaten since the days of the Guanches. They are still considered to be a delicacy.

Limpets attach themselves to the substrate, usually rocks, where they feed on algae. A by-word for intractable immobility, it is surprising to realise that, when submerged, they slowly move by wave-like muscular contractions to graze the algae. They 'clamp down' onto the rock surface with considerable force when water currents are strong or when it is exposed to sunlight at low tides. Limpets can grow old. A tagging experiment showed they can live up to 20 years.

There are four species of limpet on the Canary coast. The Fuerteventura Limpet (*Patella candei*) is endemic to the Macaronesian region, but has disappeared from all islands except Fuerteventura, the islet of Los Lobos and the Salvagen Islands (between the Canaries and Madeira). It is an endangered species, limited to certain parts of the coast, especially the protected Natural Monument Cuchillos de Vigan and Parque Natural de Jandía.

The species is protected throughout the islands during the peak months of reproduction (September to April). In some areas they cannot be harvested at all.

A limpet on the coastal rocks of the Cuchillos de Vigán (Fuerteventura). This is one of the few places where the Fuerteventura Limpet can still be found in good numbers.

sea and consists of crushed shells mixed with volcanic sands. Apart from creating a beautiful white beach, they also produced extensive dune systems, with attractive flora and birdlife (see page 41).

The black beaches are of basaltic origin. They are usually small and squeezed between cliffs. Such beaches themselves are not very attractive for naturalists, but the nearby cliffs and tidal pools certainly are (see page 85). A black beach in between two rocky headlands is almost without exception a good place to snorkel – that is if the sea currents aren't so strong as to make it dangerous.

Some beaches of Lanzarote and Fuerteventura are covered with the half-fossilized nests of *Antophora* bees that were common during the Tertiary era.

The pelagic and the underwater world

The warm and clear water of the ocean surrounding the Lanzarote and Fuerteventura supports a rich, varied, and extremely colourful underwater life. As tormented and battered by the elements the islands may seem, as exuberant and lush are their submerged foundations. In the Canary waters, over 550 species of fish have been recorded, including numerous species of ray fish, parrot fish, sharks, moray eels and barracudas. There are colourful sea snails, sea stars, sea urchins, and various corals. Also, there are dolphins, whales and sea turtles.

Obviously, all these species do not occur in the ocean at random. The life forms that are present under the surface vary with substrate (sand or rock), the physical structure of the seabed (submarine lava takes on a huge variety of shapes), water depth, light, temperature and current.

The first marine habitat you encounter when you put on your goggles and swim out from one of the black beaches is an extreme one. In the surf zone, waves wash ashore and the sand is constantly moving. For nearly all forms of life, this constant movement is too much to handle. If you move away a little from the coast (depths of about 1.5 metres), the surf is less noticeable and with good light, temperature and oxygen conditions, this can be a superbly rich zone. The best places are the rocky ones, where a variety of corrals, algae,

The three marine reserves of the eastern islands.

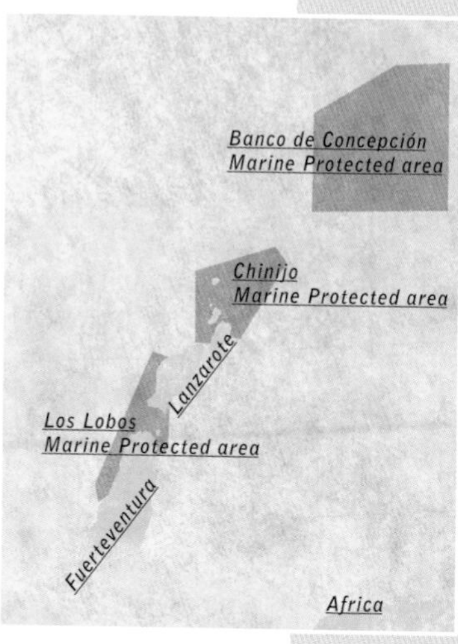

sea weeds, shellfish, sea urchins and other species can attach themselves to the sea floor. This attracts many fish.

Sandy areas are usually poorer, due to the movement of sand in the current, which prevents animals, algae or higher plants to attach themselves to the seabed. Such places are like a submerged desert. The situation is quite different where extensive sea grass beds anchor the sand. In this habitat, marine life abounds as well.

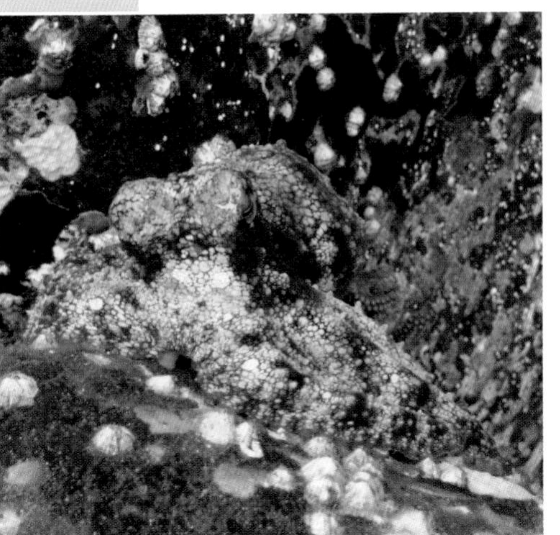

A very well camouflaged octopus.

This difference between sandy and rocky can be very striking if you happen to snorkel in a sandy area with rocky 'islands'. Swarms of colourful fish swim over these rocky bits like flies over cow dung – the sandy areas in between appear to be lifeless. This is the 'island' theory all over again (see page 21), but this time under water.

On a much larger scale, these under water islands are also present further out in the ocean. Not all submarine volcanic eruptions created islands like the current Canary Islands. Sometimes there was not enough material to show above the water line, or the material was too soft and it eroded. What remains at these places are shallow zones in the middle of the ocean. Their 'peaks' may be 50 to 200 metres below the sea level but they rise from an ocean floor that may be 3 of 4 kilometres below, so they are still formidable under water mountains.

In many areas away from the Canaries and further up to the Selvages, there are shallow parts in the ocean, and they are like islands of marine biodiversity in the midst of the ocean. Larger fish and schools of fish occur here close to the surface.

One important example is the Banco de Concepción (see map on page 35) which is not only rich in plankton and fish, but also an important feeding area for sea birds and sea mammals.

Further below in the deep sea, life becomes sparser as you sink further down and the pressure increases, the temperature drops and the light dims. The deep water is called the pelagic zone and contrasts sharply with the life-rich water near the coast.

The Canary desert

On Lanzarote, shrubby and stony desert plains and arid fields feature prominently on routes 3, 5 and 6, and site J. Expanses of sand dunes are present on route 3 and 6. Lava fields dominate in parts of route 2 and 5, and site H on page 121. On Fuerteventura you explore shrubby and stony desert plains and arid fields on routes 7, 8, 9 and 12, plis sites C and F. Sand dunes are present on route 7, 8 and 12, and above all on sites sites A (page 147) and H (page 151. 'Malpais' lava fields dominate on site B on page 147.

In how many ways can a landscape be empty? Come to Lanzarote and Fuerteventura and find out. Drive over the Tindaya plains (route 8) on a warm afternoon and the bright light, the heat, the silence and lack of life makes for a mind-numbing experience. If there is any life at all, it will be obscured by the heat haze.

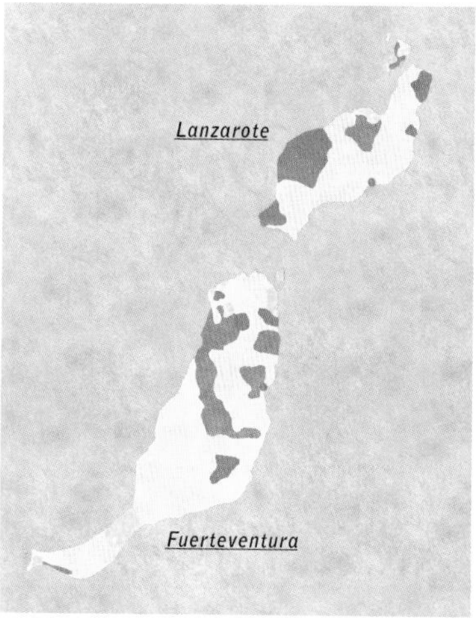

The main desert plains of Lanzarote and Fuerteventura.

But if you return late in the evening (or early morning) armed with a knowledge of the right spots gleaned from this book, you will notice that life emerges on the unforgiving desert plains.
With a little patience and close observation, you'll find the Canarian desert to be inhabited by a fascinating flora and fauna, adapted to cope with a hostile environment by keeping a low profile during the hot and dry periods and taking advantage of the cooler and moister moments.
The majority of the islands' surface is climatically a desert. However, the Canarian desert is, if you look carefully, strikingly different from that of the nearby Sahara. In fact, it has a unique flora and fauna, partly because this ecosystem developed in isolated conditions (see page 21), and partly because the ocean air evens out the temperatures and increases the moistness of the air, even if the amount of rainfall is still very low.
The Canarian desert takes on four different forms: shrubby desert on volcanic hill slopes, vast, stony plateaux with some dry, arable farmland,

Desert landscape at La Jandía (route 13).

sandy desert where rows of dunes dominate and, finally, bare lava fields or *Malpaíses*.

The shrubby desert

The shrubby desert is closest to the original vegetation of Lanzarote and Fuerteventura: rocky fields with a vegetation of cactus-like plants. None of them are true cacti, except for the introduced Prickly Pear (*Opuntia*). The cacti family naturally occurs only in the Americas, but the native flora of the Canaries uses a similar blueprint: succulence. This growth form, ideal for surviving in arid regions, also evolved in old-world plant families like the spurges (*Euphorbia*), milkweeds (*Asclepia*), composites (*Asteracea*) and goosefoots (*Chenopodia*) families. Native to the shrubby desert of the Canaries, they give rise to the term 'succulent scrub'. The wonderfully bizarre shapes of the Balsam Spurge and the Verode (a composite) are a unique and typical Canarian sight. Not all plants here are succulents, though. There are also hardy bushes like Shrubby Launaea and Canary Boxthorn.

This vegetation evolved over thousands of years in the absence of herbivores. The introduction of sheep and, especially, goats has greatly reduced the vegetation. The shrubby desert has become a lot less shrubby and a lot more desert as a result. In comparison to the lowland areas of, for example, Tenerife and Gran Canaria, the succulent scrub on Fuerteventura and Lanzarote is much less pronounced. But it hangs on in many small, lost corners in the countryside and in the hills of Bentancuria, Jandía and the mountains of Lanzarote.

In the better developed succulent scrub, the vegetation and rocky soil provide shelter for a score of small animals: geckos, skinks, lizards, grasshoppers, praying mantises, etc., all of which hide underneath leaves or between rocks and come out to hunt or forage at dusk. A walk through such vegetations at the right time of day may be very rewarding, although you need to look carefully to find the shyer animals. Top of the food chain here are the birds – especially the insect-eating species like Hoopoe, Great Grey Shrike and Kestrel, or scavengers like Raven, Buzzard and Egyptian Vulture.

The succulent scrub becomes increasingly rich in plants and animals as slopes become steeper and rockier, until you find yourself in a gully or barranco which is a different ecosystem: the thermophile scrubland (page 46-47).

The most common bush in the deserts is the Shrubby Launaea (top and bottom right). It grows virtually everywhere on both islands. You frequently come across specimens overgrown by a parasitic plant that has chosen Launaea as its host: the Alfalfa Dodder (bottom left).

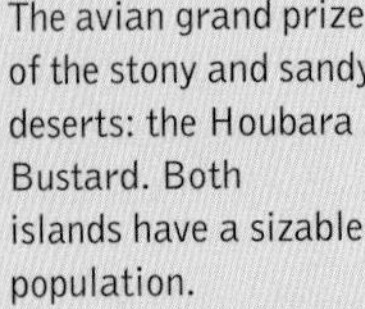

The avian grand prize of the stony and sandy deserts: the Houbara Bustard. Both islands have a sizable population.

Stony plateaux and dry arable land

On flat terrain, the original vegetation has been cleared by farmers, goats or a combination of the two. Since the arrival of humans, the area of arid plains has increased at the expense of native scrub. Such open man-made fields and natural arid desert plains (it is not always easy to tell them apart) are the favourite haunts for the true desert birds of the Canaries: Lesser Short-toed Lark, Stone Curlew, Black-bellied Sandgrouse, Cream-coloured Courser and the king of the Canarian desert: the Houbara Bustard.

The open and flat expanses of deserts are typical of the Eastern Canary Islands – you won't find them, nor their inhabitants, on the western islands. This has much to do with the age and origin of these islands. The complex volcanic activity that gave rise to these islands has created many small craters, rather than one big volcano (as on Tenerife). Over time these mountains eroded creating flat plains. Over millennia, sand filled any valleys to create a level landscape.

During the ice ages, the sea water level was much lower, leaving more land above sea level. It is estimated that the current distance between Fuerteventura and the African coast was only 50 kms during the driest period rather than c100 km as it is today. This would have made colonisation by birds easier. Hence, this landscape and its inhabitants have strong ties to the arid regions of North Africa.

Politically however, these islands are part of Spain and Spain, in turn, part of the European Union. This is important from the perspective of nature conservation, because it means that this habitat and two of its birds (Houbara Bustard and Cream-coloured Courser) are unique within the EU. This gives the area a high conservation status.

On Fuerteventura, particularly in the south, the Sodom's Apple is quite common in the desert plains. It is a highly poisonous plant, native to mainland Africa but introduced to Fuerteventura. It is an important larval food plant of Monarch butterflies.

Sandy desert and dunes

Although most of the soil is still predominantly volcanic, Lanzarote and Fuerteventura are decidedly sandier than the western islands (only Gran Canaria has a small, natural area of white dunes). Several parts of Fuerteventura are covered by dunes that fit the archetypical image of a true desert – the best being Corralejo (site B on page 147) and the La Pared isthmus (route 12 and site I on page 150).

The birdlife is sparse in these dunes. Although many of the birds (and the reptiles) that are present on the arid plains occur in the dunes as well, they do so in lower numbers. There are Houbara Bustards, Stone Curlews and Cream-coloured Coursers here, but mostly in places where there is some vegetation as well.

The vegetation of the sand dunes is unexpectedly rich. It consists mostly of thick-leaved species of the goosefoot family (*Chenopodiaceae*) – not

The most beautiful sandy deserts are at Corralejo in northern Fuerteventura.

the prettiest of plants, but one that has an outstanding track record of surviving in dry and saline environments. The most frequent shrub is Traganum, a species unique to the Macaronesian zone. In addition, there are restharrows, frankenias, the thick-leaved Canary Sea Fennel and a score of other species that will quicken the botanist's pulse.
Without these bushes, many of the plants and animals native to these environments would not survive. The extensive root system draws up the essential moisture to sustain much of the community, while the scruffy branches break the gales, offering wind-free dune slacks where animals can rest. The Atlantic Lizard and various insects seek shelter amongst the tangles, as do Spectacled Warblers.

Lava fields

The final desert type is that of the lava fields, in Spanish called Malpaís, (badlands) because they are completely unsuitable for any type of exploitation. Hence the lava fields just lie there: a large rough carpet of sharp volcanic rock in the oddest colours and most desolate shapes.
Lava fields are one of the very few landscapes that start as a biological tabula rasa, and spring into existence overnight. You can clearcut a forest or drain a lake, but organisms and seeds always remain in the soil. Only the thick carpet of red-hot lava will sweep all pre-existing life away, down to the smallest microbe. And then succession starts (see also page 21).
The potential of lava fields to form biodiverse ecosystems is great, because of the coarse structure of the lava. In most types of eruptions, lava is mixed with large amounts of gas. This gas, and the process of shrinkage as lava cools, creates a bedrock full of fissures, cracks, clefts and hollows. Ecologically, these are like millions of tiny barrancos: shady, cool, moisture -retaining shelters in a hot, dry and exposed landscape. Places into which sand, soil and seeds are easily deposited and which large herbivores cannot reach. Hence, they are a more favourable (or less hostile) place for plants to grow.
The one thing that spoils this happy image is the lack of fertile soil for plants to germinate. Soil builds up very slowly over time. Hence the actual richness of the lava fields depends strongly on their age.
Lava fields, in various stages of succession, are found both on Lanzarote and Fuerteventura. They vary from the very young, which are devoid of life, to those so far developed that the question whether they qualify as malpaís or something else becomes a moot point.
The most recent malpaíses are those of the Timanfaya region on Lanzarote (route 2). There are few places in the world where you can see

such a recent outflow of lava and a visit is a true spectacle. On this lava field, less than 300 years old, only the first signs of life, the lichens, are found. Many species of lichen occur, but only a few are the early colonisers of the bare lava. They pave the way for other species. Lichens chemically weather the rock, thereby creating a better soil for plant species to germinate. On older lava fields (such as that of La Oliva on Fuerteventura (route 8) or that of La Corona on Lanzarote (route 5), more soil has accumulated. This is where you'll find an interesting flora, in which Moon Dock, King Juba's and Balsam Spurge are key players. This is also the haunt of one of the islands' botanical highlights – the odd, cactus-like Burchard's Caralluma, endemic to Lanzarote and Fuerteventura.

The rocky cracks are also favoured places for lizards and geckos to hide. With their energy-saving metabolism, typical of reptiles, they can survive on very little food. Where the lizards and insects have settled in, the birds are sure to follow. And they bring in more seeds to germinate in the cracks of the Malpaís, thus accelerating the diversity and abundance of life.

The lava fields (top) are too rocky for the taste of most desert birds. They provide however, the perfect habitat for Eastern Canary Geckos, which occur here in high densities (bottom).

Cliffs and barrancos

On Lanzarote, splendid high cliffs and upper barranco sections feature on routes 3 and 4, plus on site E and G on pages 120-121.
On Fuerteventura, the dry cliffs and barrancos are best explored on route 8, 10, 11 and 13, plus sites F on page 149. Tamarisk thickets are part of route 8, 11 and site E on page 148. The upper barranco valleys with thermophile scrub are part of route 4 and 10 and 13.

A hugely fascinating and rich habitat is that of the wadis or, in Spanish, *barrancos*: rocky valleys cut out by water, but dry during most of the year. They only carry water directly after periods of heavy rain. The water flows quickly but leaves behind a series of slowly desiccating puddles after the torrents subside.
Naturewise, barrancos are special combining steep, rocky slopes and cliff walls with, due to the greater moisture, a lusher vegetation. That being said, it is quite hard to speak of the barranco ecosystem. Some barrancos, or sections thereof, are so wide and open that they are not at all enclosed, resembling a desert plain. In other spots, they are hemmed in by vertical cliff walls and in other places again edged by slopes giving a

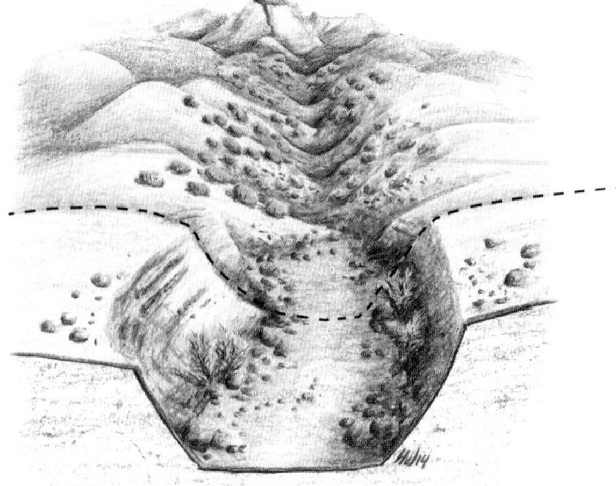

Simplified illustration of a barranco with a wide, level floor that becomes narrow and V-shaped further up. The flora and fauna in both sections is very different.

The wide lower barrancos are open and exposed, but often have patches where tamarisks can just reach the ground water. These tamarisk thickets are a magnet to songbirds.

V-shaped profile. The vegetation can be nothing more than the ordinary Launaea-boxthorn desert but may suddenly boast large thickets of Canary Tamarisks. In other places, you find yourself in a botanical hotspot, full of houseleeks, sow-thistles and other attractive wildflowers.

Depending on the terrain, each barranco section may be different, which is why hiking along barrancos is so exciting – the landscape may radically change around each bend. By and large though, you could distinguish two different sections within a barranco: the wide, exposed lower valley and the narrow, secluded one up in the hills.

The lower barranco

Barrancos tend to become wider towards the ocean, thus losing the moisture-retaining confinement of the upper barranco. Hence the flora is usually not much different from that of the plains, except for specific places, where a sudden luxuriant vegetation of tamarisks and palms marks a natural oasis!

The soils in the lower barrancos are different from the rest of the islands. The periodic streams bring down soil and sediments downhill. Rainwater sinks into these sediments and creates a freshwater aquifer which is too deep in most places to be reached by plants, other than, in some spots, the palms and tamarisks. Needless to say, these natural

The Canarian *dacotiae* subspecies of the Kestrel (note the dark plumage) is a common breeding bird of barranco walls, especially on Fuerteventura.

scrublands are a superb habitat for birds. The bird par excellence of such spots is the Sardinian Warbler. You find it almost exclusively in these places. Migrant passerines too are very much attracted to these thickets, while dragonflies use the vegetation both to rest and to establish a hunting territory for themselves.

Tamarisk thickets are frequently close to old or abandoned fields as the conditions that suit the tamarisks (underground water and better soils) are good for arable farming as well. Hence the wide lower barrancos frequently have some fields to which Hoopoes, pipits, larks and seed eating birds are drawn.

The barren rock slopes of the lower barranco, be it cliffs or steep stony hillsides, are another important bird habitat. This is particularly so for breeding sites be they for birds like Trumpeter Finch, Plain and Pallid Swift, Egyptian Vulture, Buzzard and Kestrel. It is also the preferred habitat of the Barbary Partridge and for the most exclusive bird of all: the Fuerteventura Stonechat, which is only found on that island and shows a clear preference for barranco slopes.

The upper barranco

Broadly, one could say that the lower parts of a barranco appeal to the birdwatcher, while the botanist and insect enthusiast will head for the upper reaches.

The upper barranco slopes and the high cliffs (specifically the Famara cliffs on Lazarote and La Jandía on Fuerteventura) boast a noticeably different flora than that of the rest of the islands (see also page 71). This vegetation is known as thermophile (warmth-loving) scrub or thermophile woodland. Here this name is ill-chosen, as it is by no standards a woodland and compared to the succulent scrub and desert it is thermophobe rather than thermophile. You'll only find it in places that are protected from the heat, drought and direct sunlight. The name is more fitting, though, in the context of the western islands, where this vegetation is much woodier and more exuberant, and occupies the warm slopes underneath the pine forests and laurel forests.

On Lanzarote and Fuerteventura, the 'thermophile scrub' is a bushy vegetation that occurs on the high barranco slopes and north-facing cliffs that occasionally, in winter, catch some fog and rain, and are relatively shady. An added advantage is that goats find them hard to reach.

The scrub of the upper barranco slopes and upper cliffs boast by far the largest numbers of plants endemic to the islands. It is here that you'll find the eastern island representatives of superb Canary flora: the odd cactus-like Canary Spurge, local species of houseleeks, tall flowery shrubs of viper's-bugloss, tall sow-thistles, extremely local endemic marguerites and sea-lavenders. The cliffs of Jandía on Fuerteventura and Haría on Lanzarote are museums of rare plants, including species whose entire world population grows only on that particular cliff!

On the highest, least accessible and shadiest cliffs there are even a handful of shrubs and trees that are typical of the much celebrated laurel cloud forests of the western islands. Single specimens of laurel trees like the Bosea Laurel (*Bosea yervamora*), the Canarian Laurel* (*Laurus novocanariensis*) and the Barbusano Laurel* (*Appollonias barbujana*) seem to indicate that once, there was a more luxuriant vegetation on Lanzarote and Fuerteventura. This vegetation diminished with the gradual erosion of the volcanoes, which brought the highest peaks of the islands below the altitude where clouds form on the western islands. Presumably, the final blow to this vegetation, and of many hectares of thermophile scrub and woodland, was given by Man, who cut the vegetation for firewood, and fed the rest to the goats.

The upper valleys are botanical hotspots. The succulent scrub here in a barranco near Caleta de Famara, Lanzarote, hosts a large number of attractive wildflowers, including East Canary Sow-thistle* (*Sonchus pinnatifida*) and Lanzarote Houseleek (route 3).

Human-made environments

> On Lanzarote, the only reservoir that may contain some water is the Embalse de la Mala (site F on page 120. Gardens and other well-vegetated 'oases' are in Haría (route 4) and in the resorts on the east coast. For salt pans, explore route 1 and site H on page 121.
> On Fuerteventura, the only functional but highly attractive reservoir is that of Los Molinos (route 9). The oasis-like vegetation on routes 10, 11 and 12, and sites D (page 148) and G (150) is worth to explore.

Access to fresh water is a necessity for human settlers. Permanent fresh water is lacking in most places on both Lanzarote and Fuerteventura. There were a few sources in ancient times, particularly on Fuerteventura, but they dried out. It is people's cunningness in obtaining water that is key to the development of many human-made habitats. Our gardens and plantations may all be artificial oases, but they are oases, nonetheless. Even golf courses fall into this category. They replace, at least for birds, the well-vegetated sites that were historically present on the islands but were destroyed by cutting and overgrazing.

Freshwater reservoirs

The most obvious signs of fresh water are the wells, ponds and reservoirs that, although scarce, are dotted all over Fuerteventura. The permeable bedrock of Lanzarote militates against waterbodies, natural and artificial, hence there is no surface water there.

On Fuerteventura, reservoirs were constructed in the late 20th century for drinking water and for agricultural purposes. Their shores are often bare, steep and devoid of vegetation, but where shallow, reeds appear and tamarisk thickets flourish. The water and the dense vegetation attract a new birdlife, both breeding and migratory. Coot is frequent if local, Moorhen occurs and Ruddy Shelduck, Little Egret and Cattle Egret are recent colonists that breed in small numbers. All six species of dragonfly found here are also limited to the few freshwater bodies on the island.

This is a very short list of species when compared to the lagoons of, for example, southern Spain. The poverty of the wetland flora and fauna is not only due to the fact that there is little freshwater habitat on the islands, but also because they are isolated from similar habitats. Most importantly, all waterbodies, except the Molinos reservoir (route 9) dry out annually. In fact, many reservoirs have silted up and are, at best, no more than a puddle of water. With agriculture on the islands becoming less important and drinking water now coming from desalination plants (see history section), the government is no longer maintaining these reservoirs. So fauna and flora depending on fresh water must be able to withstand periods of drought, in order to survive.

For visiting migrant birds, freshwater basins are lifesavers in a hostile desert. Migrant waders visit their shores while exhausted songbirds drop in the tamarisks to rest and find food. During warm days, the resident birds of the surrounding desert come to bathe and drink. As such, the reservoirs with fresh water are vital for all birds, even though the numbers that actually breed here, are quite small.

The reservoir at Vega de Río Palma (top) has silted up and is now virtually dry. The Embalse de los Molinos (bottom) is the only sizable permanent freshwater site on Fuerteventura.

Fields and Gardens

The irrigated gardens and plantations in villages play a similar role as the reservoirs. They are the oases of shade, coolness and moisture that many birds need. Some gardens are great 'migrant traps', meaning that many exhausted migrants land there to rest and feed. A famous one is the strip of woodland at Costa Calma (route 12), which frequently hosts rarities (including, during most winters, Olive-backed Pipit, which is unusual as this is a breeding bird of

The gardens and parks of Betancuria village are true oases and form a hotspot for songbirds and butterflies.

Golf courses, such as this one in Caleta de Fuste, Fuerteventura, are artificial oases. The grass and ponds attract many birds. Like these Ruddy Shelduck, which feed between the golfers, seemingly unhandicapped by their presence.

Siberia!). Even golf courses play this role, although in this case it is a dubious one: they provide food for migrating songbirds, but are devastating in every other sense, using up vast amounts of water and taking valuable space at the expense of the native vegetation.

The gardens have many exotic wildflowers, some of which produce a lot of nectar. Wildflower gardens are a special feature of the Canaries. Many of the planted species are native to the islands and attract lots of insects. Impressive butterflies like the Monarch are mostly seen on garden flowers. Algerian Hedgehogs and geckos are common in the parks and come out at dusk, making this a wonderful time for a stroll.

The more natural oases, such as the one of Vega de Rio Palmas (route 11) and the valley of Haria (route 4), are among the very few places to find the relict populations of Fuerteventura Blue Tit, Greenfinch, Sardinian Warbler and Canary. These species not only profit from the gardens, but also from the old fields and cultivations around the villages.

Salt pans

On the edge of the dark lava and the deep blue ocean, the salt works stand out in the landscape. Most of them are on Lanzarote (route 1, site H on page 121). There is one on Fuerteventura and another on Isla de los Lobos (route 7). Bright white cones of salt, contrast spectacularly with the dark lava and the bright blue sky. Apart from an extraordinary landscape, these salt pans are an ecosystem of their own.

Salt is used to preserve and season food. The quality of the salt from the Canary Islands is internationally highly regarded. In ancient times, it was a scarce commodity and used as currency. Roman soldiers received their pay in salt (*sal*) which is the origin of the word 'salary' (*salario* in Spanish).

Salt production is entirely based on the evaporation of sea water – a process that also takes place in salt marshes, to which the *salinas* (salt pans) as an ecosystem are akin. The old saltworks employed a complex system to pump seawater in the pans with the help of wooden windmills with cloth sails. These windmills are one of the oldest examples of the exploitation of wind energy in the Canaries. A very shallow layer of sea water was pumped into a basin (or pan) where the sun caused the water to evaporate, leaving the salt behind.

The saline mud is home to a few species of invertebrates which occur in huge numbers. They are an important food source for waders. Some interesting salt tolerant plants, such as Bassia, various saltwort species, Zygophyllum and Warty Sea-lavender* (*Limonium papillatum*) can frequently be found around the salinas.

Salt pans (top) are important as feeding areas for waders and Little Egrets (bottom).

History

On Lanzarote, the routes 2 and 4 are of interest from a historical point of view. On Fuerteventura, those of historical interest are routes 9, 10 and 11.

The early history of the Canary Islands is shrouded in mystery. Recent DNA research indicates that the earliest inhabitants arrived 2500 years ago (and perhaps a little earlier) and were of Berber stock later supplemented in Roman times. However, the first recorded visits were by Carthaginians in the 5th century BC. They mentioned that the islands were deserted, but they report finding ruins of great buildings, suggesting the islands were or had been inhabited previously. Later, the Phoenicians, Greek and Romans followed. Roman artefacts have been found, but how far there was any regular commerce with the islands in classical times is obscure. Some sources suggest the Romans or Carthaginians stayed behind, including dogs and livestock. When the Roman Empire gradually lost its grip on Western Europe and Africa, the islands sank back into oblivion. Later Arab sources did mention 'Atlantic islands' but are vague about where exactly they were, or whether they had actually visited them. It seems that it wasn't until the early 14th century that visitors returned for certain. This time contact with the outside world was to be maintained through to the present day. The Italian Lancelotto Malocello, after whom the island of Lanzarote is named, was the first to arrive and surprisingly he found a thriving indigenous population. Old chronicles tell us that inhabitants of Fuerteventura and Lanzarote were called *Maxos* (or *Mahos*) and those of Tenerife *Guanches*, but the latter name came to be applied to all these mysterious islanders. But who were these people and, more to the point, where had they come from?

The early inhabitants

Here we have the questions of island evolution all over again: since the Canary Islands are volcanic and rose from the seabed, how did these Guanches get here? This is still subject of discussion among historians and linguists. The plot thickened when it was discovered that the Guanche artefacts found – most of them on the western islands – are thousands of years old.

There are various hypotheses about the origin of the first inhabitants, including the saga of the lost civilization of Atlantis, the colonisation from Western Europe by the Celts, and the arrival of Berber ships from neighbouring Africa. There are few reports of inhabitants prior to the arrival of Lancelotto Marcello, except for that of Juba II (c50 BC – 23 AD), the Roman client king of Mauretania. Intriguingly, Juba's account notes the presence of great ruins, but apparently not of inhabitants (although it is not known how thoroughly the islands were explored). It was also this report that gave the archipelago, its name, *Canariae Insulae* or 'Islands of Dogs' since the expedition reportedly found 'great numbers of very large dogs' on the islands. It has been argued that the 'dogs' were actually *Canus marinus* or seals. This idea finds some support in the name of one of the last refuges of Monk Seals in the area – Isla de Lobos (Isle of Wolves) off Fuerteventura.

Even if the presence of numerous large feral dogs may be doubted (and no subsequent report exists of them), then the presence of other domestic animals (pigs, sheep and goats) indicates the islands weren't colonised as a result of a casual shipwreck, but by an act of deliberate policy. Although some support the hypothesis of a Celtic origin of the Guanches, DNA analyses point in the direction of tribes from nearby north-west Africa.

King Juba's finds indicate that the original vegetation on the Canaries had to cope with great predators (humans) and herbivores (their livestock) at quite an early stage, whether this was several hundreds or several thousands years BC.

What the vegetation, flora and fauna looked like before that, is not clear. Certain is that there have been many extinctions of endemic species since then, especially on the Western Islands. On Lanzarote and Fuerteventura, it is likely that much of the original vegetation was cut for fuel. This story has another curious twist. Euphorbia (spurges) which are amongst those plants that colonised and radiated on the islands, owe their name to King Juba who named the spurge, said to be a powerful laxative, after his personal physician Euphorbus. History does not record what the good doctor felt about this double-edged honour, but in 1844, the naturalists Webb and Berthelot returned the favour and honoured King Juba by naming one particular species of spurge after him: King Juba's Spurge (*Euphorbia regis-jubae*), which is quite common on Lanzarote and Fuerteventura!

The colonisation of the Spanish

When Lancellotto Malocello arrived on the islands in 1312 he not only gave his name to the island of Lanzarote, but also literally helped to put the islands on the map. Angelo Dulcert's map of 1339 was the first to show the *Insula de Lanzarotus Marocelus*: the islands would never be forgotten again.

The beautifully restored windmill of Tefia (route 8).

Soon thereafter the Portuguese Prince Henry the Navigator sponsored an expedition to the islands. Cruising the archipelago during five months, the expedition brought back the first substantive account of the islands. It mapped thirteen islands (seven major, six minor), wrote a detailed report on the Guanches and brought back four of them as prisoners. European interest in the Canaries grew quickly and new expeditions followed soon. Most of them were commercial, although the church showed interest in the islands too, with the hope of converting the natives.

The conquest of the Canary Islands took place between 1402 and 1496. The first to arrive was Jean de Béthencourt, who set off from La Rochelle, Normandy, and sailed in name of the Kingdom of Castille. The conquest was not an easy task because of heavy resistance from the Guanche aboriginals on some islands. Nor was it easy politically, given the conflicts of interest between the participants. The first conquests were carried out by Spanish noblemen purely for their private gain. Later, the Spanish Crown became interested and forced new expeditions to obtain rights to conquest in exchange for allegiance to the Crown.

The new inhabitants established themselves in the south of Lanzarote where they constructed a fortress. From this location they sailed for Fuerteventura. Hunger and a lack of resources forced the expedition to retreat to Lanzarote. The conquest of Fuerteventura finally succeeded in 1405 with the surrender of the native kings of the island.

The Castilian rule soon imposed a new economic model, mainly based on single-crop cultivation, wheat. For several centuries, the islands saw a slight but steady growth in population. Life wasn't easy in this periphery of the western world. The soil, climate and especially the lack of permanent fresh water made agriculture barely feasible. In the marginally more fertile plains, the fields were ploughed with the aid of camels. On Fuerteventura, especially, you come across many windmills constructed to grind the wheat. Some are beautifully restored (see route 9). Typically for the Canaries, the grain was first roasted. The flour made from it is called *gofio* and is still used in traditional Canarian recipes. Another

important source of food, particularly on Fuerteventura, came from goats, which converted the original shrubby vegetation into meat and milk (for cheese). What the land yielded was complemented by a modest fishery. The combination of all of this is what life on Fuerteventura was about.
On Lanzarote, Prickly Pears (*Opuntia cacti*) were cultivated to feed cochineal lice. Both the cactus and the lice were introduced from America. Dried and ground, the lice were an important natural dye. Today, such cultivations are still found near the village of Guatiza. In the region of La Geria in the south of Lanzarote, the vineyards are famous, mostly because of the unusual way of growing the grapes – each individual vine is planted separately in a hole in the ground shielded by a wall. This is the only way to grow them on a dry island as Lanzarote. It is in fact quite amazing that they grow here at all, considering that the vine is naturally a plant of riversides of southern Europe!
Despite these agricultural efforts, most of the land was too dry, poor or rocky for any crop. The larger part of the land on both islands remained (as it still is) untended, wild and unappreciated. Except, of course, by the goats. They value any greenery, regardless how remote the hillside upon which it grows.

The vineyards of Lanzarote are unique – each vine is planted in a hollow in the volcanic gravel and shielded against the wind by carefully erected stone walls (route 2).

Over the years, the human population rose steadily until the eruption of the Timanfaya volcano (see also box on page 20). The subsequent agricultural and economic disaster spurred mass emigration, primarily to the Americas during the 19th and first half of the 20th century.
After the establishment of a democratic government in Spain in 1978, the Autonomous Community of the Canary Islands has its own president, its parliament and two capitals (Las Palmas on Gran Canaria and Santa Cruz on Tenerife). Each of the seven major islands is ruled by an island council (Cabildo Insular). In 1986 Spain, and thereby the Canary Islands, joined the EU, and ushered in a new stage in the history of Lanzarote and Fuerteventura: the age of mass tourism.

The natural history of Lanzarote and Fuerteventura

It would be fascinating to know what Lanzarote and Fuerteventura looked like in distant historical times. What birds were present, and in what numbers? Was the original vegetation much denser than it is today?
Unfortunately, we have no accounts of what these islands were like when the first inhabitants arrived. The first to give a good description was the distinguished ornithologist, David Bannerman. He describes, in a visit in May and June 1913 to the eastern islands, the desert-like lands where just a few people lived:

"When I say the plain and the hills were bare, I mean they looked so from a distance, for the ground, though very parched and dry, bore a certain amount of scanty vegetation, in patches appearing almost purple from the bloom of the Suoeda fruticosa. Certainly in the neighbourhood of villages many acres are sown with wheat, but the corn is usually so poor in quality that it hardly serves to ameliorate the parched appearance of the country.
On the plains from the central ridge, which forms a broken backbone to the island, several villages are spread out, the little white houses scattered without plan over the desert waste. Perchance a cluster of date-palms indicates the homestead of one of the richer landowners, while only a few fig-trees or, maybe, a solitary pomegranate, mark some poor farmer's dwelling. Wheat and beans, vines and tomatoes, are cultivated in certain districts, while quantities of onions are exported annually from Lanzarote. ... There is not a sign of water, not a vestige of forestland nor even a wood, in the humblest sense of the word, breaks the monotony of the scene. It seems perfectly natural to have exchanged the mules of the Western Islands for camels – the only beasts of burden in the Eastern Group."

The rise of tourism

In 1960 the population of Lanzarote was 36,500, but today, that figure is 151,000. In 1960, there were virtually no tourists on Lanzarote. Currently, the number of tourists is between 1.5 and 2 million per year. The numbers for Fuerteventura are different, but the trend is the same: an explosion of the human population. Imagine the impact on the nature, landscape and culture of the islands!
The rise in population and tourism – each feeds off the other – took place almost entirely after 1985, with the biggest growth in the 1990s. There are various reasons for this sudden growth in tourism, including well-known causes like greater prosperity, cheaper flights and package deals bringing holidaying on the islands within reach of the masses. These reasons also apply to islands like Tenerife and to the Spanish mainland, but there, tourism started much earlier and took place in an area that had a much larger

And what about the birds, how abundant was bird life on the islands say, one hundred years ago? We know little, but it is again Bannerman who gives as an insight of the situation at the beginning of the 20th century:

"Though constantly on the lookout for birds, we were disappointed to find them remarkably scarce, and nothing appeared in sight but Short-toed Larks and a few Berthelot's Pipits. As we began to leave the coast, this state of affairs improved a bit; two Kestrels were spied hovering over the plain; a Koenig's Shrike was procured, but a Black-bellied Sand-grouse, flying very high, passed overhead well out of gun-shot. We soon began to skirt a wide valley, where a certain amount of cultivation had taken place-a thin creep of wheat covered a large expanse of ground, but one could easily have walked between the blades of corn without trundling upon a single one. A flock of Cream-coloured Coursers were frightened. We were now rising slowly all the time; the wide barranco, still parallel with our track, lay on our right, and it was there that we saw and obtained our first Fuerteventura Chat.
We decided to camp at a spot called Caldereta, and here we pitched our tents under the shelter of a lava-built Wall. The number of Hoopoes in this neighbourhood greatly astonished us-in every direction they were to be seen. Trumpeter Bullfinches kept visiting the old stone well for their evening drink. I was delighted to find how tame they were. Spanish Sparrows literally swarmed everywhere, filling the air with their noisy chatter as they fought and squabbled in the palm-trees nearby.
As we neared Oliva, Coursers were again seen; Pipits were common and Short-toed Larks abounded. When cactus hedges began to make their appearance, Hartert's Brown Linnets became plentiful".

native population to begin with. Lanzarote and Fuerteventura went from sleepy desert islands to booming tourist resorts within just two decades! The turning point came with the technology to thermally desalinate seawater. Fresh water has always been the main limitation to life – human or otherwise – on the eastern islands. Lanzarote built a desalinisation plant – the third in the world – in the mid-1990s. With the sudden unlimited supply of fresh water, the door opened to mass tourism. Resorts sprouted from the barren volcanic ground like mushrooms in a damp forest. Thousands of new jobs were created and new roads, tracks and 400 km of powerlines were constructed all over the islands, criss-crossing an otherwise open landscape. Hundreds of new houses, some illegally built, appeared in the landscape. In Fuerteventura the number of goats, providing meat, milk and cheese for both natives and tourists, increased from 20,000 in 1970 to nearly 120,000 at present.

Nature conservation

Like any small, isolated island with many endemic species, nature on Lanzarote and Fuerteventura is very fragile. The population size of species can be small – sometimes ridiculously so, such that they are confined to a single spot or valley. Minor ecological changes can seriously disrupt the composition of the flora and fauna of these islands.

Tree Tobacco, an invasive weed of disturbed desert plains. It is very common on both islands.

The changes that took place over the last centuries were by no means small. They were huge. When the Europeans arrived in larger numbers in 1402, Lanzarote had only 300 native souls. Six hundred years later that number has multiplied nearly a 500-fold, and that is not even counting the 2 million tourists!

The impact is obviously huge but since it is still unclear what the landscape

César Manrique designs

Born in Lanzarote, César Manrique (1919 - 1992) became a famous artist and architect and the first person on the island to work in nature conservation. Being fascinated by man´s relationship with landscape, he campaigned for the environment and sustainable tourism. In 1978 he received the World Prize for Ecology and Tourism. Today, the César Manrique Foundation keeps working on the preservation of Lanzarote´s nature and owns an art-gallery featuring art created by César Manrique himself. His works have left their mark on the island, some of the remarkable spaces designed by him are Jameos del Agua (route 5), Mirador del Río (route 4), Jardín de Cactús and the Oven-Grill Timanfaya (route 1). The César Manrique House Museum is located in the village of Haría (route 4).
www.fcmanrique.org

The Mirador del Río is a César Manrique design. Its spacious restaurant and balcony is built inside the cliff.

looked like when the first wave of Europeans settled at the beginning of the 15th century, it is hard to say what has happened to nature and landscapes during this time. To what extent Lanzarote and Fuerteventura were originally wooded, and how much of their surface was desert is unclear. What is certain is that the harvesting of shrubs and small trees for firewood and the grazing of goats has increased the area of desert. In addition, the demise of many species was caused by the introduction of predators like rats and feral cats and shooting and trapping by the new inhabitants. With the construction of roads and powerlines, and the increasing disturbance of the plains, many rare and endemic species are dangerously close to extinction – whether we talk about well-known birds as Houbara, flagship species like Jandía Spurge, or obscure things like Betancourt's Dwarf Mantis (*Pseudoyersinia betancuriae*; discovered only in 1991). In fact, given the massive changes that have taken place over the last 30 years, it is amazing how much is still present, and even quite well preserved.

Conservation efforts

The need to conserve the unique nature of these islands was recognised at a fairly early stage. In 1974 the Timanfaya National Park was created and in 1993, the whole of Lanzarote was declared a Biosphere Reserve. Pioneer nature conservation work was done in the 1980s, when comprehensive legislation was enforced prior to the mass development of facilities for tourism. Today, there are thirteen protected areas on Lanzarote

Massive real-estate projects for new tourist complexes are threatening valuable coastal ecosystems – Caleta de Fuste, Fuerteventura.

The Canary Islands didn't have any native large herbivores. The introduced goats have destroyed much of the natural vegetation. They are the curse of the vegetation, especially on Fuerteventura.

and twenty on Fuerteventura, and a total of over a third of the surface of the islands is under some kind of protection. Fuerteventura still has no National Park, but UNESCO declared part of the island, including its marine habitats, a Biosphere Reserve in 2009.

The importance of protecting the surrounding ocean has been recognised only recently. Extensive areas of the coastal waters are now marine reserves and Important Bird Areas (IBA), including the straits that separate Fuerteventura and Lanzarote, those that divide the Chinijo islands from Lanzarote, and the shallow Banco de la Concepción north of Lanzarote.

Sadly, there are recent plans (2022) by the Moroccan government to drill oil at two new oil fields halfway between the islands and the Moroccan coast.

Conservation issues on Lanzarote and Fuerteventura today are largely covered by extensive legislation. There are many nature conservation initiatives by NGOs, often in collaboration with the locals. There has been a clear change of attitude towards nature: no longer is there a poor rural population that sees shooting and egg collecting as a vital means of survival or as a way to add excitement to dull day-to-day life. The most important areas are now under protection, and efforts are being made to mitigate the negative effects of an increased population pressure. There are even voices advocating the shooting of feral goats, to alleviate the grazing pressure.

LIFE projects to save the Houbara Bustard

The Houbara Bustard, which is represented by a local race (*fuertaventurae*) on Lanzarote and Fuerteventura, is threatened worldwide. Hence its preservation is considered of highest importance. Several projects, funded by EU LIFE projects together with the Canary governments, the island Cabildos (councils), the British RSPB/BirdLife and Swarovski Optik, were launched to preserve this bird.

The projects' aims were to understand the Houbara's ecological requirements and to restore and protect its habitat. Furthermore, educational projects were run in schools, cultural centres and centres of tourism in order to raise awareness and produce a positive image of the bird. The aim was to convince landowners, police officers, gamekeepers, politicians and also tourists to be respectful to the needs of these birds.

One finding of the was that up to 17% of the population was killed in collisions with power lines. These deaths were caused – self-evidently – by the power lines but were greatly aggravated due to disturbance (by goats, farmers and tourists). Disturbance caused the birds to fly up and crash into these lines. Hence it is important that you stay on tracks, and preferably in your car, in the areas with Houbaras.

In the LIFE projects, power lines were rerouted to go around areas with high Houbara densities. Also, new areas with remnant populations are now protected.

Protected area for steppe birds (aves esteparias) on Lanzarote. Protective measures have slowed down or perhaps even halted the decrease of populations of rare steppe birds on the islands.

FLORA AND FAUNA

Lanzarote and Fuerteventura have a flora and fauna that is poor in total numbers of species but very rich in endemics – species that are confined to a very small region of the world. Much of what you find here, you'll find nowhere else, except, in some cases, on the other Canary Islands. This is what makes Lanzarote and Fuerteventura such special places. Harbouring a large number of endemics is a typical feature of islands (see below and the evolution chapter on page 21).

Since Lanzarote and Fuerteventura are so close to one another, they are biologically speaking very similar. Yet, they are also part of the Canary Island archipelago, which is in turn part of a collection of archipelagos (Canary Islands, Madeira, the Cape Verde Islands and the Azores) known as the Macaronesian region. This makes them ecologically an island within an island within an island.

This "Russian (Babuschka) doll" effect is strikingly visible when looking at the endemic species. A large portion of the flora and fauna on Lanzarote and Fuerteventura are part of the biggest 'babuschka' – that of the larger Macaronesian region. Plain Swift, Berthelot's Pipit and the Canary (the bird) are endemics on this Macaronesian level, as are many plants of the higher slopes. On Lanzarote and Fuerteventura many of these species are relatively scarce, since they are typical of the milder climates which are not well represented on the eastern Islands.

Obviously, the eastern islands share a good number of species with the other Canary Islands, (the babuschka within the babuschka of Macaronesia). Examples are Verode (Kleinia), Canary Spurge and the Canary subspecies of birds like Kestrel and Buzzard.

Since Lanzarote and Fuerteventura are much hotter and drier, they also have their own species that are not found elsewhere. The odd looking Burchard's Caralluma (see flora chapter) is an example of an East Canary endemic. Finally, at the smallest babuschka level, there are even species that occur only on one of the islands, or even only at a small part of one island. Good examples of those are the Fuerteventura Stonechat

A lone Cream-coloured Courser in the white sands of Corralejo, Fuerteventura. This is how the flora and fauna of the eastern islands manifests itself - a sudden gem, hidden in a wide and seemingly empty landscape.

(only on Fuerteventura) and the Jandía Spurge (only on the Jandía Peninsula of that same island).

Apart from the endemics, Lanzarote and Fuerteventura also share many species with arid North Africa and the Mediterranean. Being close to the continent and having a similar climate, the African influence is prominent, with species like Cream-coloured Courser, Trumpeter Finch, Houbara Bustard and Plain Tiger, a spectacular butterfly. Mediterranean species occur as well. There are many Mediterranean plants, but also birds like Sardinian and Spectacled Warblers, Lesser Short-toed Lark and Eleonora's Falcon.

Finally, there is the large group of species that have been introduced, by accident or design, by humans. Large numbers of weeds from the Mediterranean, some rodents, garden plants and goats are all newcomers to the islands. Some of them have had a huge impact on the natural world of these islands.

Endemics on the Canary islands

	Total native	Of which endemic
Higher plants	1932	522
Invertebrate fauna	7152	2835
Vertebrate fauna	110	21
Total (numbers)	9194	3378
Total (%)	100%	37%

Two endemic sea-lavenders. The Warty Sea-lavender* (top) with its typical zigzag inflorescence is restricted to two Macaronesian archipelagos, while Felty Sea-lavender* (bottom) occurs only on Lanzarote and Fuerteventura.

Introduced
Barbary Ground Squirrel
Atlantoxerus getulus
Barrancos

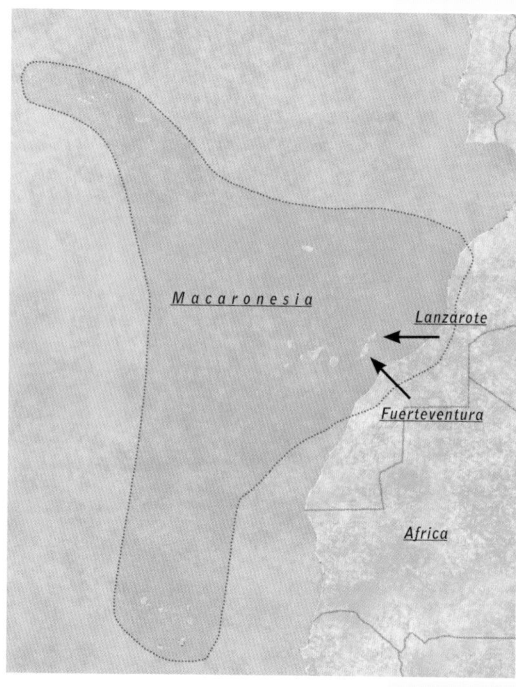

Macaronesian endemic
Berthelot's Pipit
Anthus berthelotii
All dry habitats

Eastern Island endemic
(Lanzarote and
Fuerteventura)
Burchard's Caralluma
Caralluma burchardii
Lava fields

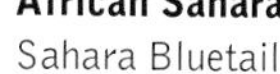

African Sahara
Sahara Bluetail
Ischnura saharensis
Temporary pools

Fuerteventura endemic
Canary Island Stonechat
Saxicola dacotiae
Barrancos

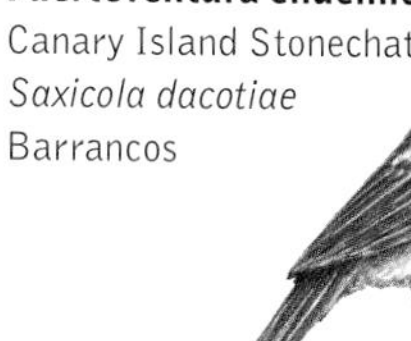

Flora

The best botanical routes on Lanzarote are route 4 and to a lesser extent, route 3. There are also interesting wildflowers to be found on the walks E, G and H on pages 120-121.
On Fuerteventura, the richest wildflower haunt is the Pico de la Zarza (route 13), but routes 7, 8, 10, 11 and 12 have interesting wildflowers to offer as well.

The flora of the Canary Islands is famous amongst botanists for its variety, spectacular and oddly shaped plants, many endemic species, and for being a refuge of a flora of humid, subtropical environments. Such environments were once widespread in the Tertiary period, but are now confined to the Atlantic islands.
This huge botanical wealth is not evenly spread across the Canary Islands, though. Unfortunately, Lanzarote and Fuerteventura are the most poorly endowed. In fact, the eastern islands are often classified as those 'where nothing grows' or as being mere 'chunks of the Sahara desert tossed into the Atlantic'. At first glance you may be seduced into believing this, but – fortunately – it is far from the truth. Lanzarote and Fuerteventura do indeed lack the lushness of the western islands, but there is still a lot to discover. In fact, they each have more endemic plant species than the entire UK!

Well-developed semi-desert vegetation on La Graciosa.

Canarian Flora

To understand the seemingly paradoxical status of the flora of the eastern islands – on the one hand poor and barren and yet, on the other, rich in endemic species – you need to consider the isolation of the Canary archipelago as a whole. As a result of this isolation, the flora abounds in endemic species that evolved on the spot from only a few ancestral species (see also evolution chapter on page 21). Hence, only few plant families occur, but many of these are present with a high variety of often endemic species. In the case of the Canary Islands, these are the spurges (*Euphorbia*), Viper's-buglosses (*Echium*), Marguerites (*Argyranthemum*), Sow-thistles (*Sonchus*), and, above all, the houseleeks, of which entire genera are completely or largely endemic to the Canaries (e.g. *Aeonium, Aichryson, Greenovia* and *Monanthes*). These groups consist of many species, each adapted to its own specific environmental condition, one of them being the hot, dry and sunny climate of Fuerteventura and Lanzarote. Isolated from their relatives on other islands, they have in turn evolved into their own proper species. The spectacular Decaisne's Viper's-bugloss* (*Echium decaisnei*) has a relatively wide range, encompassing Lanzarote, Fuerteventura and Gran Canaria, but others are more restricted: Bonnet's Viper's-bugloss* (*Echium bonnetii*) is unique to Fuerteventura; Lanzarote Viper's-bugloss* (*Echium pitardii*) is endemic to that island while Jandía Viper's-bugloss* (*Echium handiense*) is restricted to the peaks of the Jandía peninsula of Fuerteventura. Jandía Spurge* (*Euphorbia handiense*), the most cactus-like of all the Canarian spurges, has a similarly restricted range. Etcetera, etcetera. Lanzarote and Fuerteventura are not high enough to catch the moisture from the trade winds that support the laurel and pine forests of the western islands. The rich flora of these vegetation zones is absent from Lanzarote and Fuerteventura except for a handful of relict specimens that cling onto the highest north-facing cliffs of La Jandía and Famara (an indication that these forests once existed here as well).

The Shrubby Launaea is the most common and widespread shrub of both Lanzarote and Fuerteventura. It flowers year-round, but usually only with a couple of flower heads at a time.

Though largely lacking the moisture-demanding flora of the western islands, Lanzarote and Fuerteventura have their own attractions. They support a number of plants with affinities to the Mediterranean and arid regions of Africa that are rare or absent on the other Canary Islands.

To these groups belong an endemic species of Fennel, Yellow Cistanche, Opophytum (a strange relative of the ice plants) and many others. Perhaps the most typical desert plant of Lanzarote and Fuerteventura is Burchard's Caralluma – an endemic cactus-like plant of the Milkweed family that has many relatives in the mountains of northern Africa and the Middle East.

Rich plant regions and habitats

Notwithstanding this optimistic introduction, you'll find, as you drive through the interior of either of the islands, the landscape is pretty much a barren one. Except for a couple of hardy plants, most notably the spiny Shrubby Launaea* (*Launaea arborescens*), the equally thorny Canary Boxthorn* (*Lycium intricatum*), Mediterranean Saltwort (*Salsola vermiculata*), and the tall, Sodom's-apple Milkweed (*Calotropis procera*) the land is largely empty with even these plants usually looking as if they have lost hope of better times. In fact, the only plant that seems to prosper is the parasitic Alfalfa Dodder, which frequently smothers the Shrubby Launaeas. The ground-hugging Canary Aizoon and Common Ice Plant are other frequent species, as is the flimsy, two-metre-high stalk of the Tree Tobacco – an introduced species that does well on disturbed lands.

How different to this image is the natural climax vegetation: a scrubland containing a variety of succulent (thick-stemmed, water storing) bushes, in which the aforementioned Shrubby Launaea and Canary Boxthorn are common, but grow alongside spurges, viper's-buglosses, sow-thistles, houseleeks and lavenders.

A good way to understand the flora of Lanzarote and Fuerteventura is to see it as an attempt to develop from the sorry-looking Launaea-boxthorn desert into the much richer succulent scrub – an attempt that only truly succeeds in very specific places, namely old lava fields, upland areas and cliffs, and here and there along roadsides.

The Pinnate Lavender is a plant of slopes with a little shade and moisture, such as the cliffs of Famara (route 4).

The succulent flora

The succulent scrub is a typical Canary vegetation type, found on all the islands and in a small area on the nearby African coast. Because of the many endemic and succulent species, it is radically different from any Mediterranean scrub. The places where you'll find this vegetation on the eastern islands are on old lava fields (e.g. routes 2, 5 and 8) and upland areas (route 3, 4, 10 and 11). Old lava fields are too rocky to suit the needs of agriculture and are full of cracks in which plants can root. Those same cracks accumulate that little bit of soil and moisture that plants need to grow – something that is lacking in the young lava fields, which is why these are devoid of plants. The mountains, even though they barely reach over 600 metres, tend to hold clouds longer and receive a bit more rain – hence they too support a richer succulent flora. Interestingly, also roadsides frequently surprise with some wonderful patches of succulent flora. Some of these obviously have been planted, but others, especially the herbs and weeds, clearly established spontaneously.

The three main players of the succullent scrub: King Juba's Spurge with its long leaves (top), Balsam Spurge with its oblong, small leaves (centre) and Verode, which looks like a miniature tree (bottom).

The common succulents are Verode (*Kleinia neriifolia*), Balsam Spurge (*Euphorbia balsamifera*) and King-Juba's Spurge (*Euphorbia regis-jubae*; sometimes referred to as *E. obtusifolia*). The Verode looks a bit like a bonsai Dragon Tree, whereas both spurges are spherical bushes that primarily differ in the shape of their leaves. In the lava fields, they are frequently joined by Moon Dock and Zygophyllum (see page 33).

The star species of the lava fields is the rare, square-stemmed Burchard's Caralluma – one of the strangest plants of the eastern islands. It flowers only in winter and early spring. Even then, only one in hundred-or-so plants will carry the typical wine-red flowers frosted with white velvet. What's special about the Caralluma is that it is one of the very few plants on the Canaries with a true cactus growth form: no leaves and only a swollen stem that does the job of photosynthesis. On the mainland of Europe, another species of Caralluma grows in the Almería region of Spain – this is the only native cactus-like plant of the continent.

In upland areas, the flora is much richer and includes flowery bushes of lavender, marguerite (Lanzarote and Fuerteventura each have a different species), Decaisne's Viper's-bugloss, East Canary Sow-thistle* (*Sonchus pinnatifidus*) and various houseleeks (*Aeonium* and *Aichryson*). At these altitudes you'll also encounter many annual and perennial herbs, which flower in winter and early spring, such as the bright yellow Lanzarote

Wildflowers of succulent scrub of lava fields

Balsam Spurge *(Euphorbia balsamifera)*[CAN], King Juba's Spurge *(Euphorbia regis-jubae)*[CAN], Lanzarote Bird's-foot-trefoil *(Lotus lancerottensis)*[LF], Burchard's Caralluma *(Caralluma burchardii)*[LF], Thick-leaved Fluellen* *(Kickxia heterophylla)*, Pinnate Lavender *(Lavandula pinnata)*[MAC], Canary Aizoon* *(Aizoon canariense)*, Ice Plant *(Mesembryanthemum crystallinum)*, Small-leaved Ice Plant* *(Mesembryanthemum nodiflorum)*, Verode *(Kleinia neriifolia)*, Fagonia *(Fagonia cretica)*, Patellifolia *(Patellifolia patellaris)*, Moon Dock *(Rumex lunaria)*, Shrubby Heliotrope *(Heliotropium erosum)*

Wildflowers of succulent scrub of the mountains Balsam Spurge *(Euphorbia balsamifera)*[CAN], King Juba's Spurge *(Euphorbia regis-jubae)*[CAN], Canary Spurge *(Euphorbia canariensis)*, Jandía Spurge *(Euphorbia handiense)*[F], Canary Rockrose *(Helianthemum canariense)*, Thyme-leaved Rockrose *(Helianthemum thymiphyllum)*[LF], Lanzarote Viper's-bugloss *(Echium pitardii)*[L], Bonnet's Viper's-bugloss *(Echium bonnetii)*[CAN], Decaisne's Viper's-bugloss *(Echium decaisnei)*[CAN], Campylanthus *(Campylanthus salsoloides)*[CAN], Verode *(Kleinia neriifolia)*[CAN], Pastor's Asparagus* *(Asparagus pastorianus)*, Broad-leaved Squill *(Scilla latifolia)*, Rosy Garlic *(Allium roseum)*, Fagonia *(Fagonia cretica)*, East Canary Sow-thistle* *(Sonchus pinnatifidus)*[LF], Lanzarote Houseleek *(Aeonium lancerottensis)*[L], Sweet Houseleek* *(Aeonium balsamiferum)*[CAN], Lanzarote Giant Fennel* *(Ferula lancerottense)*[LF], Fuerteventura Gold-coin* *(Asteriscus sericeus)*[F], Lanzarote Gold-coin* *(Asteriscus intermedius)*[L], Common Asphodel *(Asphodelus aestivus)*, Thin-leaved Asphodel* *(Asphodelus tenuifolius)*, Willow-leaved Carline Thistle* *(Carlina salicifolia)*[MAC], Narrow-leaved Nettle* *(Forsskaolea angustifolia)*[CAN], Morroccan Reichardia* *(Reichardia tingitana)*

L = endemic to Lanzarote *F = endemic to Fuerteventura*
CAN = endemic to Canary islands *MAC = endemic to Macaronesian islands*

Bird's-foot-trefoil, the purple Fagonia, Morroccan Reichardia* (*Reichardia tingitana*; a dandelion with a dark centre of the flower-head) and the small Lanzarote Viper's-bugloss (*Echium pitardii*; replaced on Fuerteventura by Bonnet's Viper's-bugloss – *E. bonnetii*).

Flora of cliffs

Since drought and – on Fuerteventura – herbivores are the main challenges to plants, it is not surprising that the best botanical refuges are steep cliffs. The higher refuges and those facing the north are considerably less affected by drought and solar radiation. Such cliffs are found in the mountains of Betancuria and, as noted, in La Jandía on Fuerteventura and Famara on Lanzarote. These are by far the richest plant haunts, harbouring the bulk of the endemic species found on both islands.

More than 100 km apart, both the Famara and the Jandía cliffs are ecological islands in themselves. Hence the plants growing here have frequently developed into distinct species but are related to those that grow in similar conditions on the western islands. These are the groups for which the Canary flora is so famous: the houseleeks, the marguerites, the viper's-buglosses and the sow-thistles.

The spectacular Decaisne's Viper's-bugloss is an uncommon plant of well-vegetated barrancos. It is often planted as an ornamental shrub.

Wildflowers of (north-facing) cliffs

Canary Oak Fern *(Polypodium macaronesium)*, Canary Buttercup *(Ranunculus cortusifolius)* [MAC], Sycamore-leaved Mallow* *(Lavatera acerifolia)*[L], Famara Reichardia *(Reichardia famarae)*, One-styled Curry Plant *(Helichrysum monogynum)*[L], Felty Sea-lavender* *(Limonium puberulum)*[LF], East Canary Houseleek* *(Aichryson tortuosum)*[LF], Betancuria Houseleek* *(Aichryson berthencourtianum)* [F], Loose-flowered Monanthes *(Monanthes laxiflora)*[CAN], Bolle's Volutaria *(Volutaria bollei)*[LF], Jandía Viper's-bugloss *(Echium handiense)*[F], Jandía Hare's-ear *(Bupleurum handiense)*[LF], Ifloga *(Ifloga spicata)*, Winter's Marguarite* *(Argyranthemum winteri)*[F], Barbusano Laurel* *(Apollonias barbujana)*[MAC]

The Yellow Cistanche is a stout plant that parasitizes on saltworts. You will find it in dunes and saltmarshes, such as in the Isthmus de la Pared (route 12).

Flora of coasts and sandy areas

In areas where sand is the dominant stratum, or places where the salinity is higher, the flora is radically different – except of course for that threesome that just about occurs everywhere: Shrubby Launaea, Mediterranean Saltwort and Canary Boxthorn.

The most attractive plant hunting areas on sandy soils lie close to the coast. Very typical here are the big, scruffy Traganum bushes, with their thickly leaved branches sticking out to all sides (see photo on page 33). The yellow flowers of the Narrow-leaved Restharrow and the fleshy leaves of the Canary Sea Fennel are also a common sight. Interestingly, the latter is a plant of coastal rocks on the western islands – a position that is occupied on Lanzarote and Fuerteventura by the succulent Zygophyllum bush (photo on page 33). Locally, the Yellow Cistanche and the winter-flowering East Canary Sand Crocus* (*Androcymbium psammophylum*) bring an extra splash of colour to the otherwise brown landscape.

Wildflowers of sandy coasts

Traganum *(Traganum moquinii)*MAC, Orotava Saltwort *(Salsola orotavensis)*CAN, Mediterranean Saltwort *(Salsola vermiculata)*, Bassia *(Bassia tomentosa)*MAC, Broad-leaved Sandwort* *(Minuartia platyphylla)*LF, Snowy Polycarpaea* *(Polycarpaea nivea)*MAC, Bolle's Stock* *(Matthiola bolleana)*LF, Zygophyllum *(Zygophyllum fontanesii)*MAC, Narrow-leaved Restharrow *(Ononis angustissima)*, Sea-heath *(Frankenia laevis)*, Canary Sea Fennel *(Astydamia latifolia)*MAC, Warty Sea-lavender* *(Limonium papillatum)*LF, Medusa's Bindweed *(Convolvulus caput-medusae)*F+GC, Yellow Cistanche *(Cistanche pelyphaea)*, Schultz' Gold-coin* *(Asteriscus schultzii)*MAC, East Canary Sand Crocus* *(Androcymbium psammophillum)*LF

Mammals

The adorable Barbary Ground Squirrel is easy to spot on route 11, but also likely on route 8. Whales and dolphins are occasionally seen from the ferries (route 6 and site A on page 119) and from the vantage point on the eastern side of the island (site I on page 121). Algerian Hedgehogs are frequently seen as roadkill, but a walk through Costa Calma Park (route 12) at dusk may yield views of a live one.

The mammals of Lanzarote and Fuerteventura today consist of only one native bat and a single endemic shrew but there are several introduced species. The endemic Canary Shrew only lives on Fuerteventura, Lanzarote and the smaller islands of Lobos and Montaña Clara, where it inhabits lava fields and other dry land with little or no vegetation. It is very difficult to observe and there are no studies about its behaviour in the wild. The other native species is the Kuhl's Pipistrelle, a small bat of North Africa and a large part of Europe. The poverty of native land mammals is easily understood by reflecting on the island's isolation in the Atlantic. Given that the Atlantic poses less of a barrier to bats than land-based mammals, it is a little surprising to find only one species.

The mammals you are much more likely to see are those that were introduced by humans: Rabbit, Algerian Hedgehog and Barbary Ground Squirrel. The Rabbit is thought to be the first species to be introduced. It is common and widespread and has adapted well on both islands. The nocturnal Algerian Hedgehog, which differs from Common Hedgehog in being much paler and slightly smaller and slimmer, is fairly common too. You can find the hedgehog anywhere, but it is most common near habitation, where it easily finds food. It has a varied diet but a particular taste for birds' eggs. They have a negative effect on breeding populations of steppe birds, but to what extent is not well known.

The Barbary Ground Squirrel was first introduced to Fuerteventura in 1965 (it doesn't occur on Lanzarote) from the former Spanish colony of Ifni, now Moroccan territory.

The introduced Barbary Ground Squirrel is an adorable animal and exploits its looks very effectively. In some places, the population lives off bread and nuts fed to them by tourists (route 11).

It adapted well to the island's arid conditions. In the 1980s their numbers were estimated to exceed 300,000. Over the last decades the population has dropped somewhat but it is still the most visible wild mammal on the island. The Barbary Ground Squirrel lives in groups of 15 to 20 animals. They are active during the cooler time of day and take, in true Spanish fashion, a siesta between about 13:00 and 15:00, before becoming active again. Other introduced mammals are Black and Brown Rats and House Mouse.

The Algerian Hedgehog is nocturnal. You may come across it on an evening stroll through parks or gardens.

The Lava Mouse

The Lava Mouse (*Malpaisomys insularis*) is an extinct endemic rodent from the Eastern Canary islands. Its fossil remains have been found in cavities in lava fields of Lanzarote, Fuerteventura and Graciosa. The species went extinct probably following the arrival of the first humans, the Guanches, who introduced dogs (a predator) and the House Mouse (a competitor).

On calm days you have a good chance of seeing Bottlenose Dolphins from the ferry between the islands.

Marine mammals

The waters around the Canary Islands are rich in marine mammals. So far, 29 species of cetaceans (dolphins and whales) have been recorded. The Canary Islands mark the southern limit of distribution for cold water species and the northern limit for those of tropical water, which explains the presence of such a wide variety of species. Unfortunately, this does not mean the islands are the best places to actually watch dolphins and whales. Only from the ferry or on (infrequently) organised whale-watching trips can the smaller species, in particular Common and Bottlenose Dolphins, be frequently seen.

Isla sin Lobos – What happened to the Mediterranean Monk Seal?

Known by the Spanish as the Sea Wolf (*Lobo del Mar*), the Mediterranean Monk Seal gave name to the islet *Isla de Lobos* off the coast of Fuerteventura. Once, seal colonies were numerous on the Canary Islands. There were several thousands of animals when the Spanish settled here, but soon they were hunted to extinction for their fur, meat and fat.

Today, the Mediterranean Monk Seal is one of the most endangered mammals in the world. Of their original range from the Black Sea to the waters of the Canaries, there are only two main populations left: one in the Aegean Sea of Greece, and a smaller one of about 120 individuals in the Eastern Atlantic. The latter is centred around Madeira and the shores of Morocco and Mauritania.

The first known description of the Mediterranean Monk Seal dates back to Aristotle. The animal was depicted on one of the first coins ever, minted around 500 BC. It must have been abundant at that time. Disturbance, conflict with fishermen, entanglement with their nets and pressure on food supplies all played a role in the species' decline, but the coup de grace was the development of tourism in the 20th century. The beaches of the Mediterranean quickly filled with people, expelling the Monk Seal from its breeding areas, leaving only inaccessible undersea caves to give birth to the young.

At present, Monk Seals are only occasional visitors in Lanzarote and Fuerteventura's coastal waters. The animals probably come from the neighbouring colony of Madeira. The four countries that control the seal's Atlantic population (Spain, Morocco, Mauritania and Portugal) have now started to develop an Action Plan for the recovery of the species. One of the main elements of the plan will be to create a network of Special Areas of Conservation, comprising of marine and coastal reserves. In 1996 the IUCN (International Union for the Conservation of Nature), classified the Monk Seal as 'Critically Endangered', but the conservation measures in the first decades of the millennium, the Monk Seal is beginning to recover. Numbers went from an al time low of only 500 individuals to about 700 today. In 2015, the IUCN changed the animal's status to a 'hopeful' Endangered (so without the 'Critical'), and there is hope that one day the Monk Seal can come back to inhabit *Isla los Lobos* once again.

A diorama specimen of the Monk Seal (taken in the Natural History Museum of Milan).

Birds

The best routes for finding steppe birds such as Houbara are route 3 (on Lanzarote) and 8, 9 and site C on page 148 (on Fuerteventura). Waders are best on route 1 and sites F and H on page 121 (Lanzarote) and routes 7, 9 and 12 on Fuerteventura. Barranco and cliff breeders are best seen on route 4 and 6 and site G (page 121) on Lanzarote, and routes 8, 9, 11, 12 and site E (page 148) on Fuerteventura. The species seen in barrancos and cliffs on Fuerteventura are rather different than those on Lanzarote. Sea birds are best (in season!) on route 6 and site I (page 121) on Lanzarote, and routes 7, 8 and 12 on Fuerteventura. The ferry between both islands (site A on page 119) may also prove rewarding.

It was not until the 1990s that Lanzarote and Fuerteventura became a popular destination for birdwatchers. Before that, the poor tourism infrastructure made travel difficult. Today the wide availability of comfortable hotels, increased accessibility and the convenience of pleasant distractions for non-birding companions while you are off chasing birds, makes it a top destination.

The variety and quantity of birds is not spectacular, but the quality is excellent with one species, the eponymously named Fuerteventura Stonechat, that you won't find anywhere else on the world. Other

The Berthelot's Pipit is the most common bird of the Canary Islands. You'll find it in any open, dry vegetation.

interesting species include the (local subspecies of) Houbara Bustard, Barbary Partridge, Cream-Coloured Courser, Lesser Short-toed Lark, Spectacled Warbler, Trumpeter Finch, Barbary and Eleonora's Falcons, to name but a few. Lanzarote and Fuerteventura together form one leg of the dual birding hotspot of the Canaries. The others are Tenerife and La Gomera (for which we've written a separate Crossbill Guide).

The birdlife of Lanzarote and Fuerteventura is very different from that of the other Canary dream destinations. In comparison, Lanzarote and Fuerteventura have a range of desert birds that you won't find on the western islands. Additionally, the islands attract many migrants and vagrant birds and hold a unique collection of rare sea birds (although the latter may be difficult to see). However, many of the Canarian forest birds, such as Canary and the local variety of African Blue Tit, are rare on Lanzarote and Fuerteventura.

Though most birdwatchers come during the winter to escape the bad weather back home, the characteristic species can be found year-round, and the mornings are always the best time to be in the field.

Without doubt, the desert plains and the rocky barrancos are the two habitats that have most of the sought-after species to offer. In desert lands, such as these islands, the few places with fresh water attract birds like a magnet. This applies to all oases, including gardens and golf courses. Finally, the coast, with its tidal pools, patches of salt marsh and the open expanse of ocean itself, are other important birding habitats.

Lanzarote and Fuerteventura's birdlife in a nutshell

Canary and Macaronesian endemics Barolo Shearwater, White-faced Storm-petrel, Madeiran Storm-petrel, Plain Swift, Berthelot's Pipit, Fuerteventura Stonechat, African Blue Tit, Canary

North-African and Mediterranean species Ruddy Shelduck, Cattle Egret, Little Egret, Egyptian Vulture, Eleonora's Falcon, Barbary Falcon, Barbary Partridge, Houbara Bustard, Cream-coloured Courser, Black-bellied Sandgrouse, Pallid Swift, Turtle Dove, Hoopoe, Lesser Short-toed Lark, Spectacled Warbler, Sardinian Warbler, Great Grey Shrike, Spanish Sparrow, Trumpeter Finch

Other specialities Bulwer's Petrel, Cory's Shearwater, Manx Shearwater, Storm-petrel, Red-billed Tropicbird, Osprey, a variety of migrant waders and vagrants from Europe, Africa and North-America

Exotics Sacred Ibis, Hadada Ibis, Monk Parakeet, Red-vented Bulbul, African Collared Dove, Laughing Dove

The subspecies *koenigi* of the Iberian Grey Shrike is endemic to the Canary Islands. It is common on Fuerteventura and frequent on Lanzarote, but rare on the western islands.

Bird subspecies and their characteristics

There is a passionate and ongoing debate, whether some populations of birds are separate species, subspecies, or a mere variety within a larger population. Canarian birds are a great example in this debate because many of them show clear differences from the 'default' species (the *nominate*, in ornithological jargon).

Here is a list of the subspecies of Lanzarote and Fuerteventura and in how they differ from the 'standard' European or African race. In all these cases the mentioned subspecies is the only type that occurs on the islands.

Egyptian Vulture (Canary subspecies *majorensis*) – Reddish and grey shades
Sparrowhawk (Macaronesia subspecies *granti*) – Smaller and darker
Buzzard (Canary subspecies *insularum*) – Smaller, lighter, underside more streaked
Common Kestrel (Canary subspecies *dacotiae*) – Darker, males head darker grey
Houbara Bustard (Canary subspecies *fuerteventurae*) – smaller, darker back with more spots
Stone Curlew (Canary subspecies *insularum*) – pinkish, more heavily streaked
Yellow-legged Gull (Macaronesian subspecies *atlantis*) – Smaller, darker
Barn Owl (Canary subspecies *gracilirostris*) – underparts darker, yellowish
Lesser Short-toed Lark (Canary subspecies *polatzeki*) – more sandy-rufous in colour, no striped flank
African Blue Tit (East Canary subspecies *degener*) – paler and greyer, dark stripes on head narrower, underparts paler yellow and single wing bar
Great Grey Shrike (Canary subspecies *koenigi*) – Smaller with dark flanks
Raven (Canary/African subspecies *tingitanus*) – Much smaller, higher call, brownish plumage

Birds of desert plains

The community of birds of the desert and semidesert plains consists of only a few species, but these are spectacular. The dry, open plains are home to Houbara Bustard, Cream-colored Courser, Stone Curlew, Black-bellied Sandgrouse and Lesser Short-toed Lark, with a 'supporting cast' of more widespread species like Barbary Partridge, Spectacled Warbler, Trumpeter Finch, Berthelot´s Pipit, Hoopoe, Kestrel, Buzzard and Great Grey Shrike.

The Houbara Bustard is distributed over a large area stretching from the Canary Islands to Egypt (The Middle-eastern population is now considered a different species, the Macqueen's Bustard).

Over much of its range, the Houbara is threatened with extinction. The most significant threat is hunting by rich Arab falconers, for whom the Houbara is the grand prize. The highest densities of this magnificent bird are present on the Eastern Canary Islands.

Lanzarote and Fuerteventura house – of course – a separate subspecies, Chlamydotis undulata fuertaventurae. DNA studies showed that the population has been completely isolated from the African populations for 20 – 25,000 years. The total population on the islands is only around 600 birds, of which c450 live in the central plain of Lanzarote and nearly 150 in various areas in Fuerteventura. There are also a few birds on La Graciosa. Since the population on Lanzarote is restricted to just a small area, the densities here are by far the highest. Houbara prefer level or only slightly undulating, not too rocky terrain, and are very sensitive to disturbance. Visitors in late winter and early spring may enjoy the spectacular display of the Houbara, in which the males raise their white breast feathers and bury their neck and head in them, making them look like a pompom on legs.

The Houbara's habitat preferences are shared by Cream-coloured Courser, Stone Curlew and Black-bellied Sandgrouse. The Cream-coloured Courser feeds on ground insects, which it captures by making short sprints. It prefers the more stony or sandier plains. On the islands, the Cream-coloured Courser occupies a larger area, but occurs in lower densities than the Houbara.

The Stone Curlew is a bird of the stony plains and dunes but can equally be seen around goat pens and even near urban areas. It is not rare, just hard to spot when it sits still on the ground. In the evening its unique call can be heard everywhere.

The characteristic flight call of the Black-bellied Sandgrouse is the best way to discover this magnificent bird. It is closely associated with fields and is the rarest of the desert plain birds on the islands.

Various 'LBJs' (little brown jobs) can be found on the plains. The most frequent is Berthelot's Pipit which is widely distributed all over Lanzarote and Fuerteventura as it is on other Canary Islands. It can be seen in all open areas with little vegetation, even on lava fields. Lesser Short-toed Lark is equally abundant. Outside the breeding season it congregates in groups that wander over the plains. The Trumpeter Finch, perhaps more a 'little pink job', is a very gregarious bird, which also congregates in flocks after the breeding season. They breed in the rocky terrain, but frequently

The Cream-coloured Courser is widespread on desert plains. It is equally at home in sandy as in stony deserts. Though not uncommon, it takes time and dedication to pick it out it on the wide plains.

feed in fields and around goat pens. Often it forms mixed groups with Short-toed Larks, Spanish Sparrows and Linnets.

Birds of rocky slopes, barrancos and cliffs

Most of the surface of both islands that doesn't fall into the category of 'desert plain', are dry rocky slopes, barrancos (gullies) or cliffs.

Your average rocky slope will appear to be devoid of birds, but if you look or listen with care, you will encounter Berthelot's Pipit, the occasional Trumpeter Finch, a lone Hoopoe, a chatty Spectacled Warbler or watchful Great Grey Shrike. And all of this is overseen by the local Kestrel, Buzzard or Raven.

The Fuerteventura Stonechat (see box on page 82) is principally a bird of steeper slopes and barrancos. Here and there you may also see it as well on stone walls or more gentle rock slopes. This bird is only found on Fuerteventura where it is common. It feeds on insects caught on the ground or in the air and is quite approachable. If you just walk quietly through the ravines and scan the rocks, you should find it without a problem.

The sheltered barrancos are bird hotspots. They are not only the best places to see the chat, but also to track down Barbary Partridge. This bird, introduced in many places in the world, is native to the Canary Islands and North-Africa. Its population fluctuates due to hunting pressure. In spring you can hear the distinctive song of males even at great distances. After the breeding season, they form small family groups.

With plenty of holes, barrancos are great for cavity breeders. Both Plain Swift and Pallid Swift breed in the crags of steep cliffs. It is easy to see their dizzying flights, capturing insects in the air. Both species are present from March to October, but a few Plain Swifts usually hang around in winter.

Most Trumpeter Finches also breed in barrancos, as do Sardinian Warblers in places where tall bushes are present. The Ravens, Kestrels and Buzzards that roam all over the islands, mostly breed in inaccessible barranco slopes, as does the rather scarce Barn Owl (yet another bird that is represented with an endemic subspecies).

Egyptian Vultures prefer to breed on the steeper cliffs. The local race is distinctly smaller, darker and more colourful than the Egyptian Vultures on the mainland. It feeds mainly on carrion from goats. Although it has virtually disappeared from the rest of the islands, on Fuerteventura there is a stable population thanks to the abundant livestock. Rock Doves also breed on cliff ledges, as does its main predator, the fearsome Barbary Falcon.

The Barbary Partridge is a widespread but uncommon bird of the islands. It prefers scrubby hillsides.

The Barbary Falcon is a bird most easily encountered on Lanzarote. It breeds on the Famara cliffs (route 4).

Fuerteventura Stonechat

The Fuerteventura Stonechat is a sedentary bird that only occurs on Fuerteventura. It moves only over short distances – that is, only the juveniles do, probably in search of new territories or better food conditions. Bizarrely for a species that is perfectly capable of flight, sightings on nearby Lanzarote are extremely rare, even though there is plenty of apparently good habitat available here.

The Fuerteventura Stonechat prefers dry slopes in stony ravines with over 15% of shrub coverage. It seeks out places with lots of big stones and rocks and avoids sandy and pebbly terrain. The presence of abundant lookouts from where to localise its prey is important, as well as the presence of insects and other invertebrates.

Male Canary Island Chat.

It is believed that the Fuerteventura Stonechat population is declining, due to overgrazing and extensive construction projects. However, we have no numerical information about population trends, with the only accurate count from 2010 placing the population size at 13.400-15.500 pairs.

Seabirds and cliff breeders

Lanzarote and the small and inaccessible islands of the Chinijo Archipelago to the north are hugely important to the nesting sea birds. Many species that occur here are unique to the Atlantic islands of Macaronesia (Canaries, Cape Verde Islands, the Selvages, Madeira and the Azores).

The seabird colonies of these islands are very different from those in the northern Atlantic. There are no excrement-caked cliffs stacked with noisy gulls and auks here. Instead, the colonies are quiet, almost secretive, where birds come in at night and leave for the open ocean again in the morning.

The most common sea bird, apart from Yellow-legged Gull, is Cory´s Shearwater. It breeds commonly on the rocky coasts of Lanzarote, Fuerteventura and the smaller islands, and even in barranco cliffs further inland. This is the only pelagic (oceanic) species that is found

without much difficulty from the coast and from the ferries. Bulwer´s Petrel and Barolo Shearwater (the latter endemic to the Macaronesian islands) breed in some numbers on Lanzarote. They are seen occasionally from ferries, but a pelagic birdwatching trip is the best way to find them (see page 122). The highest numbers breed on the islands of the Chinijo Archipelago, where they form mixed colonies with White-faced Storm-petrel, Madeiran Storm-petrel and European Storm-petrel.
The recent arrival of the stunning Red-billed Tropicbird adds an exotic spice to the mix. It first started breeding in 2013, and in 2018 there were up to 11 nests, most of them in a small colony on Fuerteventura (with 15-23 individuals present). This bird, originally only known from tropical oceans, is now seen fairly regularly off the coast of Lanzarote and Fuerteventura.
Apart from these true sea birds, there are a number of other breeding birds of coastal cliffs. Osprey and Eleonora's Falcon both exclusively breed on coastal cliffs. Eleonora's Falcon is a colonial breeder and has its prime Atlantic population (c85 pairs) on the islands of the Chinijo archipelago and Famara cliffs (the only other colony is on the Moroccan coast). This elegant falcon has specialised on hunting migratory songbirds, which are easy prey when they arrive exhausted on land after a sea crossing. Consequently, it nests late in the year. The Osprey preys on fish. In contrast to the populations in northern Europe, the local Ospreys hunt in the coastal waters of the ocean. Barbary Falcons, Ravens and Rock Doves are not exclusively found on sea cliffs, but do not ignore the opportunities to nest and feed here.
In winter and during migration, skuas, Gannets and terns visit the waters around Lanzarote and Fuerteventura, albeit in low numbers (see page 162).

Birds of beaches and rocky coasts

The coastal fringe of the islands makes for poor breeding grounds but offers a lot of food for migrating birds. Breeding birds include only Yellow-legged Gull, Little Ringed and Kentish Plovers, but there are a lot of other birds to see in autumn, winter and spring.
Many wintering and migrating waders show little fear and with patience they can offer good opportunities for photography. Apart from Kentish, you will frequently come across Whimbrel, Grey and Ringed Plovers, Knot, Greenshank, Common and Green Sandpiper. Turnstones live in small flocks and are perhaps the most common of the waders. They are even present in summer.

Observation periods of breeding seabirds on the Canary Islands

Species	Population	Observation period	Location
Cory´s Shearwater	> 1000	Feb - mid Nov	all islands
Barolo Shearwater	< 1000	Jan - Dec	Chinijo
Bulwer´s Petrel	~ 1000	Feb - Sept	All Islands except Fuerteventura
White-faced Storm-petrel	< 100	Feb - June	Montaña Clara
European Storm-petrel	> 1000	June - Oct	Alegranza
Madeiran Storm-petrel	< 1000	late Sept - mid Feb	Lanzarote, Chinijo
Yellow-legged Gull	> 1000	Jan - Dec	all islands
Red-billed Tropicbird	< 50	mostly Sept	Chinijo/ Fuerteventura

Increasingly reported in recent years, the breeding of Red-billed Tropicbird on the Canary Islands was finally confirmed on Lanzarote in 2013, but it remains a very rare bird.

Sanderling is a winter visitor and passage migrant. Little flocks play catch chase with the foam along the beaches in morning and in the evening when there are not too many people about. The beaches and sand banks off the coast attract the same birds. The most frequent tern is the Sandwich Tern which is found both in winter and during migration. It is often found in small numbers, resting on beaches or patrolling the nearby surf. On migration, numbers in excess of a thousand are sometimes recorded.

Birds of salt pans and reservoirs

Of the few wetlands that may attract waders, the saltpans on Lanzarote are the most important. Many of the waders mentioned in the previous paragraph also occur on the salt pans, and often in higher densities. In addition, this is the place to add Black-winged Stilt, Little Egret, Little Stint and stray rarities to your list.

Whereas salt pans are found on Lanzarote and Isla de Lobos, the freshwater reservoirs are typical of Fuerteventura. Many of them are not maintained and have silted up, but the main reservoir, that of Los Molinos (route 9) attracts many birds. The fact that it is artificial, doesn't deter the birds. The Coot is

Two common waders in winter and during migration: the Grey Plover (top) frequents rocky coasts, while flocks of Sanderling (bottom) can be found on quiet sandy beaches.

The silent islands – extinctions on Lanzarote and Fuerteventura

In recent times, three Canarian birds, one full species and two subspecies, have become extinct. The Canary Black Oystercatcher (Haematopus meadewaldoi) once roamed the coasts of the eastern islands. It was endemic to Fuerteventura, Lanzarote and the Chinijo archipelago (the islands north of Lanzarote). It was a resident bird that has never been recorded outside this area. Only four birds were ever collected, the last one being on La Graciosa on June 3, 1913. The naturalist Bannerman published a lithograph of this bird (reproduce here) and wrote about the event:

"For fear of disturbing the bird, in case it should still be about, we crawled the last fifty yards through the prickly scrubs. Eagerly we scanned the black rocks, which here run some way out to sea, and suddenly the sharp eyes of our guide spotted the bird. It was feeding not a hundred yards below where we were lying, running nimbly over the rocks. As I raised my head, the bird got up, uttering a sharp 'peepe-peepe, peepe-peepe', twice repeated. It was a long shot, but I dared not risk allowing the Oystercatcher to leave the island, so fired on my knees, and to my intense joy the bird fell into the sea".

Canarian Oystercatcher Artwork by Henrik Gronvold (1858–1940)

The locals of La Graciosa reported it until around 1940. In the mid-1980s a large survey was held on all the islands of the Chinijo archipelago, but failed to find any evidence of the species' survival. It is unclear what tipped the bird into extinction. Probably the population was naturally small

the most common breeding bird, with the largest population in the reservoir of Los Molinos. It is a recent colonizer with highest numbers in the winter. The Moorhen is also frequent.

More exciting is the Ruddy Shelduck, which started to breed on Fuerteventura in 1994 and now has a firmly established breeding population. Today it can be found all around the island, even far away from water. It has also profited from the establishment of golf courses with their fresh green grass.

Most inland reservoirs and the deeper barrancos, dry or not, have a fringe of tamarisks and other large plants. Both Little Egret and Cattle Egret breed in such places. The shrubs are the favourite haunts of Sardinian

and vulnerable, and hunting and overharvesting of limpets, the bird's main food source, pushed it over the edge. The final twist in the tale is that in 2019 a DNA test suggested this bird was probably not a full species but a subspecies of Eurasian Oystercatcher.

Another loss for the Chinijo archipelago is the disappearance of the 'Chinijo Chat' a local race of the Fuerteventura Stonechat, which only lived on the islets of Alegranza and Montaña Clara. This is puzzling, since no chats have been found breeding on Lanzarote and La Graciosa which lie between these small islets and Fuerteventura where the Fuerteventura Stonechat breeds. This is despite the availability of apparently suitable habitat. Perhaps the eruption of the Timanfaya volcanoes on Lanzarote are responsible for the gap in distribution of this chat. The Chinijo form became extinct in the early 20th century, perhaps due to the introduction of predators or goats.

Finally, the Lanzarote race of the recently 'split' Canary Islands Chiffchaff (*exsul*) was unique to the relatively moist Haria valley, were it persisted into the 1980s. It probably became extinct when the natural habitat of shrubby vegetation disappeared due to a combination of goat herding, agriculture and increasing aridity. Haría and Betancuria are among the few places where another bird of shrubs and trees occurs: the East Canary race of the African Blue Tit. Hopefully, this bird won't meet the same fate as the Chiffchaff.

Saxicola dacotiae murielae
Artwork by Henrik Gronvold (1858–1940)

Warbler and also attract many migratory songbirds. When water levels drop, the exposed muddy puddles attract migrating Greenshank and Common Sandpiper. These too are especially common in winter, at which time small, temporary pools form in many barrancos.

Birds of agricultural land, oases and gardens

Villages are natural oases on both islands. The gardens and small parks, with their tall vegetation provide shelter to many birds, while the surrounding fields, some of which are irrigated, provide food. Corn, figs, almonds or vines are cultivated, all on a small scale. This rural idyll is home to Linnets, Corn Buntings, Spanish Sparrows and Iberian Grey

Shrike. Look carefully among the doves. Collared Dove is very common, but Turtle Dove occurs in the summer months and Laughing Dove and African Collared Dove are also present in small numbers. The striking Hoopoe is widely distributed over the islands, but most common in and around agricultural lands.

The secretive Quail is also tied to agricultural land. Its numbers fluctuate enormously. In springs following relatively wet winters, the crops are doing well and Quails are quite common. In other years, they are almost absent.

Closer to villages with gardens and groups of palm trees, you'll encounter more members of the finch family. Linnet, Greenfinch and Goldfinch may be seen, although the latter two are quite rare. This is also the place to look for that most famous of all the Macaronesian endemic birds: the Canary. This wild predecessor of the familiar cage bird is very common on the western islands, but arrived on Fuerteventura and Lanzarote relatively recently. Its distribution seems to be restricted to some of the moister valleys with high shrubs and some tourist resorts. The gaps between the leaf stubs of palm trees are a favourite nesting site of the Spanish Sparrow, the only sparrow species on the island. They form noisy groups in most settlements, although there are also colonies in uninhabited places. Outside the breeding season they spread out over the islands looking for food on the plains.

Villages and Gardens are favoured by Plain Swifts, Pallid Swifts, Collared Doves, Sardinian Warblers and the Fuerteventura Blue Tit. The latter is

The Spanish Sparrow is the only sparrow species of the islands.

the rarest of the four Canarian subspecies of the African Blue Tit. It lives mainly in the valleys of, Betancuria (Fuerteventura) and Haría (Lanzarote), but it may be seen in other areas in low numbers. The Blackcaps you encounter here are mostly over-wintering European birds. The Macaronesian *heineken* subspecies, which is so common on the western islands, may only very occasionally nest on the islands.

Finally, in some tourist centres you may come across Laughing Doves, Monk Parakeets, Red-vented Bulbuls and Sacred Ibis. The Laughing Dove is sometimes present in large gardens but is not very abundant. It has recently been established on the islands, but its origin is not entirely clear. It could have escaped from captivity, but also could have reached the islands by itself from the nearby African coast. The Monk Parakeet is certainly an exotic species that escaped from captivity. The only stable population on Fuerteventura is concentrated in the tourist resort of Morro Jable on the Jandía penisnsula. On Lanzarote it can be found in some tourist resorts.

Two birds of the rural countryside of Lanzarote and Fuerteventura: Laughing Dove (top) and Hoopoe (bottom).

Reptiles

Eastern Canary Geckos are quite common in rocky areas, and most easily found by turning stones (they often cling to the underside of the rock you turn). The Atlantic Lizard is very common in many places, while the introduced Gran Canaria Giant Lizard occurs (but appears to be rare) in the Barranco del Torre (site E on page 148). The best chance of finding the rare and secretive Eastern Canary Skink is on route 11.

There are 14 species of reptiles on the Canary Islands, three of which occur on Lanzarote and Fuerteventura: a gecko, a skink and a lizard. In fact, all islands have a gecko, a skink and a lizard, each one closely related to those on the other islands.

The gecko is the Eastern Canary Gecko, endemic to Lanzarote and Fuerteventura. It is abundant on both islands. It even enters houses and, with luck, some geckos may move into your holiday apartment or local restaurant and lurk behind the lamp, waiting for an endemic Canary fly for dinner. Because of its nocturnal habits, it is rarely seen in the field except when you actively search for it.

The Atlantic Lizard is the only native lizard of the islands. It is common in all habitats. This is a female. The males are larger and darker.

The Eastern Canary Skink (again endemic to Lanzarote, Fuerteventura and the islet of Los Lobos) is the largest of the Canary Islands' skinks. It can reach 25 cm but, in spite of its length, it is very hard to find. More than the other reptiles, it tends to avoid extreme heat, which is quite strong on the eastern Canary Islands. Therefore, it spends much of its life underground or in rock crevices. It has a scattered distribution over the three islands. On Fuerteventura, it only occurs in the humid valleys (relatively speaking) of the centre (between Vega de Rio Palma and Betancuria), near Timijiraque and La Oliva and on Jandía. On Lanzarote it occurs around the valley of Haría.

In contrast, the Atlantic Lizard is widespread, abundant and highly visible on both islands and the nearby small islets. It occurs in all habitats from sea level up to the peaks. The Atlantic Lizard is of the genus *Galiota*, which is endemic to the Canary Islands. Galiotas are bulky animals, and some species have made it to true giants. The largest species lived on Tenerife and almost reached 1.5 metres. That one is extinct, but the species currently living on Gran Canaria measures almost a metre. This is all quite spectacular, but even more remarkable is the difference in average size of the various closely related species are. The Atlantic Lizard, the one found on Lanzarote and Fuerteventura, is the smallest of them all, the males measuring only a bit more than a Sand Lizard.

To find the Eastern Canary Gecko you need to – carefully – turn rocks in lava fields. In contrast to lizards, they usually stick to the underside of those rocks.

The Atlantic Lizard is omnivorous, feeding on invertebrates, seeds and flowers and becomes quite tame in gardens and holiday resorts. They are active throughout the year. The lizards are a so-called keystone species: an animal that plays a key role in the (original) ecosystem. On the one hand, it was (before the introduction of goats, rabbits and squirrels) the main herbivore on the islands, and on the other hand, it is staple food for Kestrels, Buzzards, Ravens and Great Grey Shrikes.

Marine turtles

Two species of marine turtle are found in the waters around the Canary Islands. The most common of these is the Loggerhead Turtle, an oceanic species distributed throughout the world. The Leatherback Turtle, the largest of all living turtles, is only sporadically seen. None of them is now known to lay eggs on the islands, and so those seen in the Canarian waters are usually migrating.

Loggerhead Turtles once bred on Fuerteventura though, and there is a program to re-introduce them. After two centuries of absence, turtle eggs were brought from the Cape Verde Islands and put in nests on the beach in Cofete (Jandía, Fuerteventura). When the eggs hatched, the baby turtles were taken to a nursery in Morro Jable for 2 years. Between 2010 and 2013, 700 baby turtles have been released on Cofete beach, and it is hoped that they will return in 15 years and lay their own eggs on this beach.

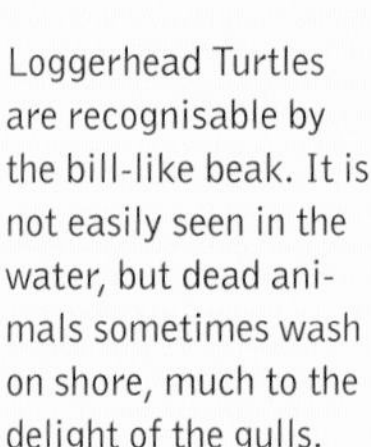

Loggerhead Turtles are recognisable by the bill-like beak. It is not easily seen in the water, but dead animals sometimes wash on shore, much to the delight of the gulls.

Insects and other invertebrates

The better vegetated areas attract most insects. Good butterfly haunts are found on route 4, 5 and 6, and site G (page 121) on Lanzarote. On Fuerteventura, route 10 and 11 are most rewarding. The flowery parks of route 10 and site G on page 150 attract butterflies like Monarch. The best dragonfly sites are routes 9 and 11 on Fuerteventura. On Lanzarote, the Famara cliffs (route 4), have a number of other interesting invertebrates.

The list of insects and other invertebrates on the islands is quite short but holds a few very interesting species. There is still very little known about the invertebrates of the islands. As late as 2012, a new species of beetle, *Tarphius jandiensis*, was discovered in la Jandía.
Insects and invertebrates are active throughout the year, but spring appears the time that the density and activity is highest.

Butterflies

Only 19 species of butterfly are found on Lanzarote and Fuerteventura. That isn't many, but there are a few you won't find anywhere but here. Early spring is the best time for most of them. Good numbers of a variety of 'whites' inhabit the dry hills. Most of them are the familiar Bath Whites and Small Whites, but among them are a number of real treats. One of them is the Fuerteventura Green-striped White, a small butterfly with distinctly pointed wings and clear green stripes on its underwings. It is endemic to Fuerteventura where it flies over fields in the valleys, like those in Betancuria (route 10 and 11). Another one is the Greenish Black-tip, a small butterfly that is

The Greenish Black-tip is native to Africa and the east Canary Islands, with just two small populations in mainland Spain.

widespread in arid Africa. It looks a bit like a cross between a Bath White and a Clouded Yellow. Both the Green-striped White and the Greenish Black-tip are found on stony slopes with sufficient nectar plants.

These sites are also the places to look for the blues, four species of which occur on the islands (Long-tailed, Lang's Short-tailed, African Grass and Common Blues). More colourful butterflies are attracted to flowery patches, such as oases and gardens. Here you may find the resident Canary Red Admiral which has a wing pattern subtly different from the familiar Red Admiral (a migrant here). Both are attracted to flowers with lots of nectar.

A few ornamental garden plants in a village are usually enough to attract the tiny Geranium Bronze (an accidental introduction from southern Africa). You need a little more luck to find the impressive orange Monarch – a large butterfly that flies around in large gardens and parks. It is the same species as

Monarch (left) and Plain Tiger (right) are both common butterflies, at least in some years. Both feed on plants of the milkweed family such as Sodom's Apple Milkweed (right).

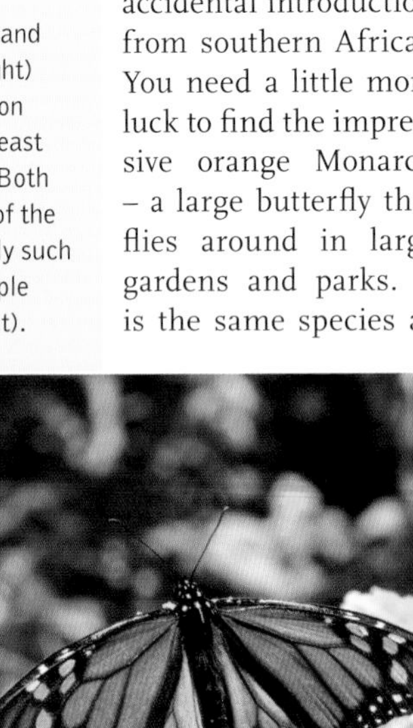

Lanzarote and Fuerteventura butterfly species

	L	F	
Large White *(Pieris brassicae)*	X	-	migrant
Small White *(Pieris rapae)*	X	X	All year
Bath White *(Pontia daplidice)*	X	X	All year
Greenish Black-tip *(Euchloe charlonia)*	X	X	Dec.-June
Fuerteventura Green-striped White *(Euchloe belemia)*	-	X	Dec.-June
Clouded Yellow *(Colias crocea)*	X	X	All year
African Migrant *(Catopsilia florella)*	X	X	All year
Monarch *(Danaus plexippus)*	-	X	Migrant
Plain Tiger *(Danaus chrysippus)*	-	X	All year
Red Admiral *(Vanessa atalanta)*	X	X	All year
Canary Admiral *(Vanessa vulcania)*	-	X	All year
Painted Lady *(Vanessa cardui)*	X	X	All year
Meadow Brown *(Maniola jurtina)*	X	-	Migrant?, march-sept.
Geranium Bronze *(Cacyreus marshalli)*	-	X	All year
Small Copper *(Lycaena phlaeas)*	X	X	All year
Long-tailed Blue *(Lampides boeticus)*	X	X	All year
Lang's Short-tailed Blue *(Leptotes pirithous)*	-	X	All year
African Grass Blue *(Zizeeria knysna)*	X	X	All year
Common Blue *(Polyommatus icarus)*	X	X	All year

L: Lanzarote F: Fuerteventura

the North American butterfly which is famous for its long migration to Mexico where it winters in enormous densities in trees. The population in the Canary Islands doesn't undertake such impressive journeys. It is a resident that can be seen throughout the year.

Its slightly smaller relative and look-alike the Plain Tiger is widespread and common in Africa, but quite rare on the Canary Islands. The small resident population is reinforced periodically by migrants from the mainland and can, at times, be abundant. Another butterfly that has erratic influxes into Lanzarote and Fuerteventura is the African Migrant. An aptly named butterfly – if they arrive on the islands, they usually do so in large numbers. There are accounts of hundreds of them invading the park of Costa Calma (route 12) overnight.

Search carefully among the dry shrubs and you'll encounter some wonderful creatures of the African desert, like this White-eyed Grasshopper* (*Dericorys lobata*; top). The female (bottom) is very different, but can be recognised by the lobed thorax.

Dragonflies

Despite the ability of dragonflies to fly long distances, there are only few species on the Canary islands. Only twelve species occur in, or regularly migrate to, the Canaries, of which no more than six occur on Fuerteventura and four on Lanzarote.

On Fuerteventura, the Los Molinos (route 9) and Las Peñitas reservoirs (route 11) are well-known sites, but sometimes dragonflies are also encountered in gorges elsewhere on the islands. Broad Scarlet and Red-veined Darter are widespread species, occurring quite far from water. Sahara Bluetail and Blue Emperor are frequent at freshwater sites, while Lesser Emperor and Epaulet Skimmer are quite rare. Most species can be on the wing throughout the year but are most numerous in spring.

Other invertebrates

There are a few invertebrates other than butterflies and dragonflies that catch the attention, and imagination. Flowers, particularly in gardens, sometimes attract the pretty, zebra-patterned bees of the genus *Amegilla*. They are sometimes joined by a similarly coloured, but differently patterned species, the Cuckoo Bee, that parasitizes on Amegilla bees' nests.

In the succulent scrub, there is a series of other curious insects. One of them is the Purpurarian Stick Grasshopper (*Purpuraria erna*), which is listed as Vulnerable on the IUCN Red List. This species occurs on Fuerteventura, Isla de Lobos, Lanzarote and Isla de Montaña Clara and feeds exclusively on spurges. There are also several praying mantises on the islands. The stout, broad-bodied *Blepharopsis mendica* is perhaps the most impressive. The small and extremely rare *Pseudoyersinia betancuriae* is endemic to Fuerteventura. The big Egyptian Locust is one of the few grasshoppers that are conspicuous in winter. It is an impressive beast. In some years, hundreds of thousands of them are caught by the wind and whisked from the African mainland to the islands, much to the dismay of farmers and inhabitants.

Most of these insects are part of the exclusive fauna of the succulent scrub that is unique to these islands. Without exception, the disappearance of this scrubland due to cutting, grazing and urban development has put a great strain on the insect life. It has pushed some species right up to the edge of extinction.

Another African species, the Praying *Mantis Blepharopsis* mendica, is a terrific insect that shows itself most frequently in the summer months. It hunts its prey from bushes. The top photo is of an adult which measures up to 8 cms; the bottom one is of a nymph (juvenile).

PRACTICAL PART

Lanzarote and the Chinijo Archipelago

Lanzarote is about half the size of Fuerteventura and is dominated by slaty-black lava. The south-eastern part is much affected by tourism and new real estate projects, but the western and northern parts (making up roughly two thirds of the surface) are still more or less untouched. This part of Lanzarote consists of three rather different areas. In the south is the impressive, barren volcanic landscape of Timanfaya National Park (route 2). North of that lies the central plain, which is home to the island's large population of Houbaras and other desert birds (route 3). North of the plains lies the long row of Famara cliffs and nearby hills, which are much greener and support most wildflowers and insects (route 4 and 5).

Just north of Lanzarote is the Chinijo Archipelago, which consists of six small islands: La Graciosa, Famara, Roque del Oeste, Roque del Este, Montaña Clara and Alegranza. The whole archipelago is now a Natural Park. Only La Graciosa, the largest island and closest to Lanzarote, is inhabited and can be visited (route 6). A visit is very much worth it: the quietude, landscape and flora are great, and the birdlife is good as well.

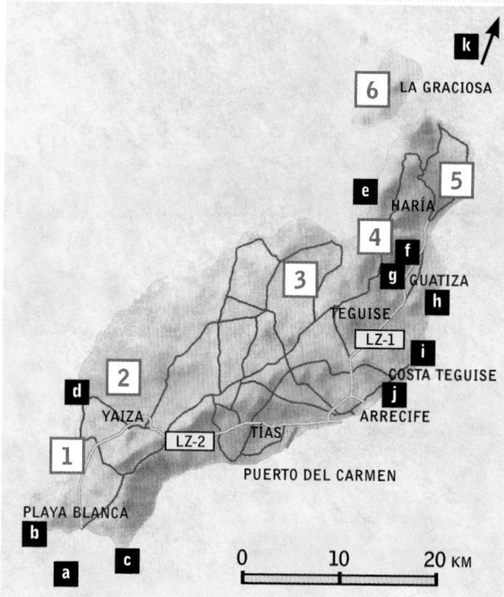

Note that on none of the routes, you'll find much shade. When doing longer walks, make sure you have protection against the sun (including sunglasses) and sufficient water with you.

There are various good sites for snorkelling, birdwatching and more, shown in the map here and described on page 119 onwards.

Birdwatching on La Graciosa (route 6).

Route 1: Salinas de Janubio

2-3 HOURS
EASY

! A telescope comes in handy

Extensive area of salt pans, excellent for migrating birds.

Habitats: Salt pans and tidal lagoon.
Selected species: Little Egret, Black-winged Stilt, Avocet, Greenshank, Ringed Plover, Kentish Plover, Trumpeter Finch, Eastern Canary Gecko

The saltpans of *Salinas de Janubio* probably have the highest diversity of birds within the entire Canary Islands. The site consists of a tidal lagoon with adjacent saltpans, both of which attract good numbers of migratory shorebirds. The population is constantly changing, with daily arrivals and departures of migrants, making repeated visits worthwhile.
The most frequent waders are Kentish and Little Ringed Plovers, both of which breed. Black-winged Stilt breeds in some years, but there are usually quite a few around. Other frequent birds are Common Sandpiper, Grey Plover, Black-tailed and Bar-tailed Godwit, Greenshank, Avocet, Dunlin and Little Stint. Hoopoe, Trumpeter Finch and Lesser Short-toed Lark breed in the drier parts of the area. 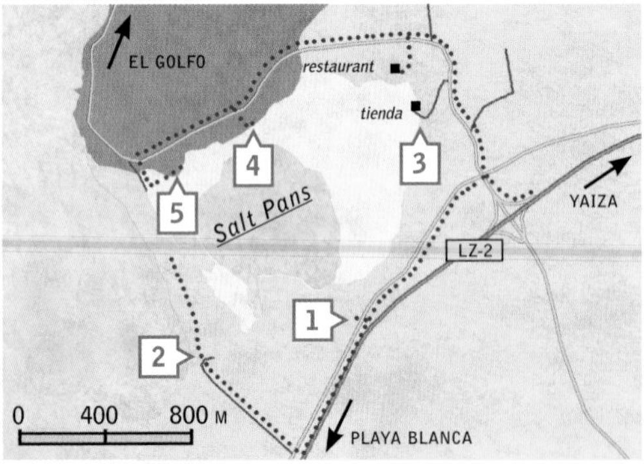
A visit to the salinas is not just about species you see. The saltpans are still in use, and the white mountains of salt with the dark brown strings of lava on the hills in the background and the black sandy beach at the coast, make for an atmospheric landscape.

Starting point Coming off the LZ-2, take the exit El Golfo, and subsequently follow the signs *Salinas de Janubio*. At the roundabout (GPS 28.938002, -13.815388), go left, direction Playa Blanca.

1 After 800 metres, just after a crash barrier, there is a car park and vantage point on your right. From here you watch over the southern part of the *salinas* and tidal pool. This spot is good for waders, and the light is good most of the day. A telescope is needed for good views.

2 Continue and after 700 metres, turn right at the sign la playa. A dirt track takes you down to a gravel bar that separates the sea from the lagoon. This site is usually best for gulls and sea birds. As you're looking north, the light is always good.

Return to the roundabout and go left, direction El Golfo. Then turn left towards the Salinas de Janubio shop.

3 Form the car park you have good views over the eastern *salinas*, which may be scanned again for waders. Alternatively, a bit further along the road, there is the Salinas restaurant, from where you also have good views. Best light conditions are in the morning.

4 Another 800m further along the road, there is a small layby on the left that offers views from the north. People often walk down to the saltpans, which is (at the time of writing) in practice allowed although formally forbidden.

5 The final viewpoint is another 600m along. Turn left at the bend of the road to enter a large car park, from where you can walk down to the salinas and the gravel bar.

Additional remark

Salina de Janubio can be combined as a day-trip with route 2 or a visit to El Golfo (site D on page 119).

The Salinas de Janubio are a delight for waders (bottom). Black-winged Stilts are usually present (top).

Route 2: Timanfaya National Park

4-5 HOURS, 40 KM
MODERATE

One of the world's most impressive volcanic landscapes. Witness the gradual recolonisation of new land.

Habitats: Malpaís, both very recent and older lava fields
Selected species: Moon Dock* (*Rumex lunaria*), Balsam Spurge, *Stereocaulon vesuvianum lichen*, Raven, Rock Pigeon

!
Entrance tickets mandatory

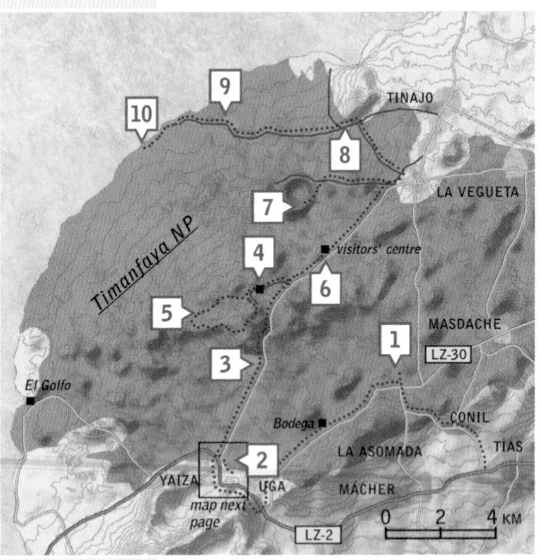

Prepare for one of the most barren landscapes you have ever seen. Timanfaya is dominated by a recent (in geological terms) lava field that resulted from an eruption in 1730. The big draw of this route is undoubtedly the otherworldly landscape (a cliché, but one that is certainly true). This route also offers you the unique opportunity to have a peek in nature's laboratory where, slowly, ecosystems are forming on brand new land. Lichens dominate the landscape – the only bush you'll see frequently is the Moon Dock* (*Rumex lunaria*), the first coloniser among the higher plants.

This route combines a visit to the National Park (points 4 & 5; entry ticket required, to be bought on site) with a walk and various short stops just outside the reserve. These are freely accessible.

Starting point Tias

Take the exit of the LZ-2 motorway direction Conil. Follow this road until you arrive at a T-junction with the LZ-30. Park on the track opposite this T-junction.

1 Take a look at the unique vineyards of Lanzarote, in which each vine is planted in a pit surrounded by a wall, to shield the plant from the desiccating wind and to enable irrigation. The plants are growing in a 'soil' of pure *lapilli* (volcanic gravel) from volcanic eruptions. The large spaces between the particles reduce evaporation and keeps the deeper soil moist. This odd landscape of pit in a row is unique to Lanzarote designed to allow crop growth in an extremely arid environment.

Turn south towards Yaiza. After almost 3 km there is a bodega, from which you have another great view over the vineyards. Continue towards Yaiza. Just before the village, follow Playa Blanca and immediately afterwards, turn right to Timanfaya NP. Immediately thereafter, turn right (GPS: 28.958377, -13.757512). Park here and explore the walking route (see small map).

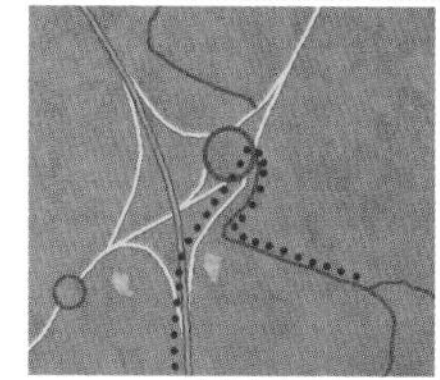

2 Following the track for a hundred metres or so, you have your first good views of the lichen-clad lava fields of Timanfaya. The species *Stereocaulum vesuviamum* (the leafy grey one) and *Ramalia* (stringy grey) are particularly common, while you need to search a little harder for *Rocella tinctoria* (dark brown, stringy with white spots) which is the most important ingredient for making the famous litmus pH tests we all used in high school.

Follow the road towards Timanfaya through a stunning volcanic landscape, where, unfortunately, you cannot park.

3 The first place to stop is the camel car park on the left side of the road – the spot where guided camel rides depart. There is not much to see here, but it is a good place to take in the landscape for a while, and to photograph some very tame Rock Doves and Berthelot's Pipits.

The next stop is the Montañas del Fuego. The entrance fee is € 12,00 per

The lava fields are covered in lichens such as this Stereocaulum vesuvianum (top). The pretty Rocella tinctoria (bottom) is a little harder to find. It usually grows in the shade of an overhanging rock.

adult (2021 prices) and worth it, since it is the only way to see the most spectacular part of the park.

4 Follow the road to the café-restaurant 2 km ahead. In front of the restaurant, you can witness the mountain spitting out its famous geysers thanks to the unusual temperatures in the sub-soil surface, caused by a magma chamber close to the surface. It is not a natural geyser of course (for that you'd need surface water) but created by staff who pour in water into the holes to create a fountain of hot water seconds later. The nearby restaurant roasts meat and *papas arrugadas* (potatoes) over a hole in the ground.

5 Take a bus ride (highly recommended and included in your entry ticket) of about half an hour through the heart of the National Park, complete with commentary in Spanish, German and English and accompanied by dramatic music. The scenery is sublime if barren except for lichens and the occasional Moon Dock* bushes. You pass fields of ropey lava and block lava, craters, and the *Islote de Hilario*, an 'island' of old lava, which has more plant cover.

Afterwards, return to the main road (exiting the park) and turn left.

6 After 3,5 km, the centro de interpretación (open 9 to 17 h. all year) has a good exhibition on the National Park.

Hues of colour around a crater in Timanfaya.

Continue and just before you reach the first houses of Tinajo, where the road bends to the right, turn a sharp left (walking sign *Montaña Caldereta*). Continue until you reach the lava fields where you can park (GPS: 29.043712, -13.701494).

7 Rated by some as the most impressive walk on Lanzarote, the trail to the Corona Blanca

(white crown) is your best opportunity to explore the young lava fields and craters of Lanzarote. This is a 3-hour, fairly strenuous walk (no shade!) through some of the most barren landscapes in the world. The first, rather lengthy part of this walk, runs through black, desolate lava fields. First you pass a small whitish crater before arriving at the main one, which you can climb and walk along its rim. The views here are spectacular!
Return along the same track.

Drive back to the junction and instead of taking the main road into the village, turn left and at the next junction (400 metres) left again. Follow this road until you reach a T-junction in front of a steep hill. Turn left and stop at the stone quarry for some botanising (29.061282, -13.711493).

8 There are a couple of interesting plant species in the roadside here, including the Lanzarote endemics Lanzarote Gold-coin* (*Asteriscus intermedius*) and Lanzarote Viper's-bugloss (*Echium pitardii*), growing together with Fagonia and Shrubby Launaea. Also, note the extremely sharp limit of young black lava (devoid of plants) and the older and lighter lava fields, which have a rich growth.

The dark fields of young lava contrast sharply with the 'islotes' of older, shrub-covered grounds.
On the foreground a Balsam Spurge.

Continue. Where the tarmac road bends to the right, continue straight onto a well-maintained dirt track.

9 You pass through the black lava fields until suddenly you arrive at another textbook example of an *islote*. Older lava, much lighter in colour, is covered with the bushes of Balsam and King Juba's Spurges. The plants grow right up to, and not a millimetre further than, the razor-sharp line where the young lava starts.

10 Continue to the end point of the track at the coast (GPS: 29.062266, -13.773575). The rough coastline can be followed on foot. The black lava contrasts sharply with the blue ocean and the white foam. Just beneath the car park is a rock arch – a beautiful example of how the soft lava erodes at the coast.
In terms of life, there is not much around, but the odd wader resting on the rocks, and some succulent Zygophyllum growing in sheltered places on the shoreline.

Route 3: The plains of El Jable

5 HOURS, 32 KM
MODERATE

The best place in Lanzarote for steppe birds.
The splendid Famara cliffs with their rich flora.

Habitats: semi-desert plains, dunes, succulent scrub, cliffs
Selected species: Traganum, Lanzarote Houseleek, Houbara Bustard, Stone Curlew, Cream-coloured Courser, Lesser Short-toed Lark, Barbary Falcon, Eastern Canary Gecko

! Part of this route passes along dirt tracks

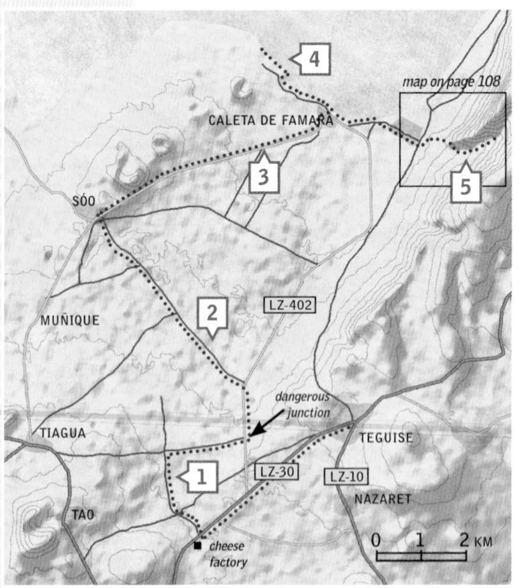

The El Jable plain in central Lanzarote is the place to see Houbara Bustard and other desert birds on Lanzarote. This trip is designed to find these birds. It follows a track in the southern part of the plains, where dry fields and natural semi-desert attract large numbers of them. Visit early in the morning when the light is best and the birds most active. Afterwards, the route takes you to the Famara cliffs where pristine sand dunes and cliffs are excellent for wildflowers and insects. Teguise, the start point of this route, is the ancient capital of Lanzarote, and is now a lovely, restored village.

Note that this is a very fragile area as it holds the largest population of the endangered Houbara Bustards on the Canaries and possibly the world (incredible but true – new holiday apartments are still being constructed in the middle of this sensitive habitat!).

Starting point Teguise

The sandy plains are the main site for desert birds on Lanzarote.

Follow the LZ-30 towards San Bartalomé, passing two roundabouts. After the second, in front of the turn left to Nazaret, turn right onto a track (GPS: 29.039333, -13.591574).

1 Drive carefully along the track, going right at the next junction, which will bring you to the tarmacked LZ-402. This itinerary is drivable (with care) with a normal vehicle (sidetracks should be ignored, both to prevent the disturbance of the birds and for the risk of getting stuck with your vehicle).
Make many stops to scan the fields and shrubby desert plains for Houbara Bustards, Stone Curlew, flocks of Lesser Short-toed Larks, Trumpeter Finches and Great Grey Shrike. Cream-coloured Coursers are about but may prove difficult to find. Flat areas with a little bit of vegetation form the best habitat for birds.

Turn left at the LZ-402, drive for 1.8 kms over in the first bend to the right, turn off on a track that goes left (GPS: 29.065318, -13.584970).

2 This track cuts straight through the plains to the village of Sóo. Make plenty of stops again to watch for birds. Note that this is a very fragile area. Don't disturb the birds and don't leave your vehicle. The bustards, in particular, are sensitive to movements of people, but less so of cars.

When you arrive at the village of Sóo, go right on the LZ-410 towards Caleta de Famara.

Stone Curlews are common, albeit hard to find. They are most easily discovered through their mournful calls at dusk.

3 There are a few places where you can stop and park, mainly at the entrance of dirt tracks. From here, scan the surroundings for bustards and other birds. There area is more dune-like, which is very good for Houbara.

In Caleta, turn left on the village main street, which turns into a track and ends at a car park on the western end.

The bulk of Lanzarote's Houbaras live on the central plains (top). Lesser Short-toed Lark is frequent in El Jable (bottom).

4 The dunes here have a few interesting plants, while there are often some waders on the rocks on the coast.

Return and follow the main street in eastern direction. Outside the village, keep left on the minor road along the beach and drive towards the *Urbanización Famara*, a square-shaped area of housing. Stay on the right side of the housing and drive all the way up and park (GPS 29.111125, -13.545415). Continue on foot up the trail that leads up the mountain towards the barranco.

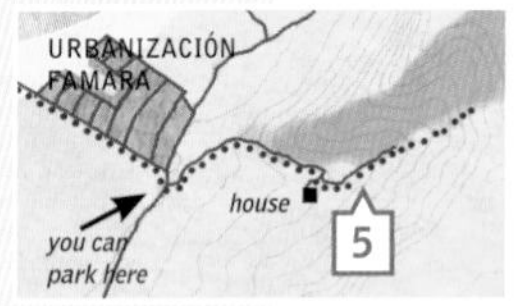

5 This trail is of interest for the view, because of the many wildflowers, lizards and geckos, but also just for the joy of a beautiful walk. It is also great to see how the landscape changes as you walk into the barranco. The first part, up to the houses, is exposed and rather dull. Beyond it, you enter a barranco that is sheltered on three sides, and here you will find an interesting flora. Verode, Balsam and King Juba's Spurge, are common on the entire slope, but as you move up, you'll find Lanzarote Houseleek* (*Aeonium lancerottense*), East Canary Sow-thistle* (*Sonchus pinnatifidus*), Pinnate lavender* (*Lavandula pinnata*) and the endemic composite *Reichardia famarae*, and various other bushes to be increasingly common. The best part of the gorge starts where the track ends and a path continues.

Route 4: The Famara cliffs

FULL DAY
35 KM

Spectacular landscape and exquisite views over the Chinijo Islands.
Home to nearly all endemic wildflowers of Lanzarote.
Attractive birdlife.

Habitats: cliffs, thermophile scrub, succulent scrub, malpaís, coast
Selected species: Lanzarote Fennel, Lanzarote Nauplius, Descainse's Viper's-bugloss, Lanzarote Houseleek, Barbary Falcon, Eleonora's Falcon, African Blue Tit, Canary, Greenish Blacktip

This route brings you to the spectacular Famara Cliffs in the north of Lanzarote – a product of millennia of erosion of the soft volcanic rock by the ocean. The high cliffs catch more rain from the northeasterly winds; hence the area is greener and more inviting than the rest of Lanzarote. This area hosts most of the islands' interesting plants. The views from the miradores on the cliffs are spectacular, especially the last one, which overlooks the island of La Graciosa (Route 6). The Famara cliffs are home to a couple of sought-after birds, while the countryside supports some birds that are common on the western islands, but rare on Lanzarote and Fuerteventura.

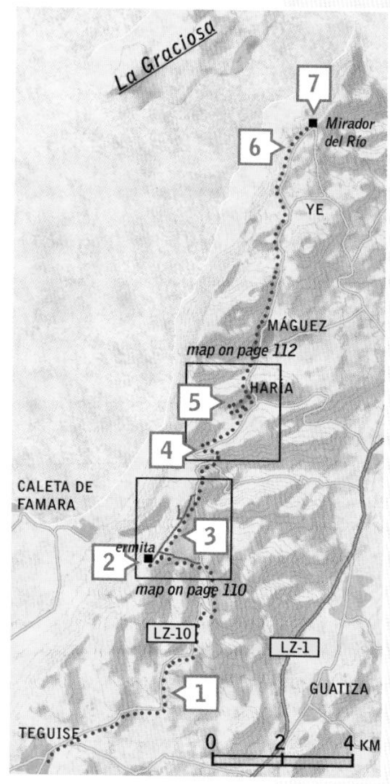

Starting point Teguise.
Head north via the LZ-10, direction Haría and Mirador del Río.

1 Immediately after leaving Teguise, you'll notice that the landscape is greener than on southern Lanzarote, with terraced fields and flowers and bushes beside the road. Don't spend much time here – there's better ahead.

An early morning in January on the viewpoint of La Ermita, overlooking the central plains of route 3. The cliffs to the right are one of the most attractive botanical sites of the island.

After the village of Los Valles, turn left to the Ermita de las Nieves. Drive on to the viewpoint just behind the Ermita (GPS: 29.106356, -13.528636).

2 From the viewpoint you have superb vistas over the central plains (the goal of route 3), the beaches of Caleta, and, towards the north, the islands of La Graciosa and Montaña Clara. With a little luck you may already see one of the raptors here – Kestrel, Barbary Falcon, Egyptian Vulture and, in summer, Eleonora's Falcon are all present. Walk towards the cliffs and (carefully!) look around for some of the more attractive wildflowers of the island. Pinnate Lavender (*Lavendula pinnata*), Lanzarote Giant Fennel* (*Ferula lancerottensis*), Lanzarote Gold-coin* (*Asteriscus intermedius*), East Canary Houseleek* (*Aichryson tortuosum*), Naked Stonecrop* (*Sedum nudum*) and Canary Buttercup (*Ranunculus cortusifolius*) are some of the attractions.

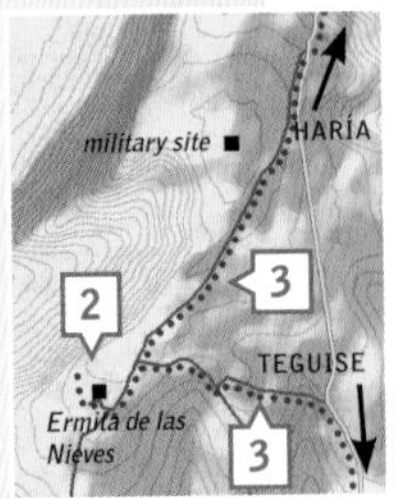

3 Take some time to explore the small roads towards and beyond the Ermita. Birds like Great Grey Shrike, Hoopoe, Linnet and Short-toed Lark (winter) can be around. In spring and summer, this may be a good place to look for butterflies (e.g. Greenish Blacktip) and praying mantises. Lizards and geckos are certainly around.

Continue in the direction of Haría. Before the village, you pass a restaurant and a group of pines, before a sharp hairpin. Park immediately beyond the hairpin on the right side of the road (GPS: 29.131318, -13.516832).

4 Carefully explore the road sections shown on the map. This area of pines is a favourite haunt of the African Blue Tit. Corn Bunting and Greenfinch (both very scarce on the islands), have been seen here as well. This road section is very rich in wildflowers, with Lanzarote Houseleek, East Canary Sow-thistle*, Lanzarote Giant Fennel*, Lanzarote Gold-coin*, Brown Bluebell, Rosy Garlic, Willow-leaved Carline Thistle* (*Carlina salicifolia*), Thick-leaved Fuellen* (*Kickxia heterophyllos*) and Lanzarote (*Echium pitardii*) and Decaisne's Viper's-buglosses (*E. decaisnei*).

!

Be careful of traffic here

Continue to Haría and park somewhere in the village.

5 Haría is a lovely, authentic village – a nice change from the uninspiring coastal towns of Lanzarote. It has a great number of vestiges of its past, aboriginal sites and traditional houses.
It is situated in a sheltered valley on the oldest formation of the island. This is the greenest part of Lanzarote, with an abundance of Canary Island Date Palms.
In and around the village, you have a good chance on finding Canary, Linnet, Greenfinch, Spectacled Warbler, Kestrel, African Blue Tit, Chiffchaff, (wintering northern birds; the endemic Canary Islands Chiffchaff that once lived in the valley is extinct on Lanzarote). Also, keep an eye (and ear, since the calls are distinctive) out for African Collared Doves amongst the many Eurasian Collareds. The dry riverbed that runs through the village, is a good place to look for butterflies.
There are several tracks you can explore, of which we recommend the one on the inset map: find the main *Plaza de Constitución* and walk the Calle la Longuera in eastern direction, past the library, straight on until it turns into a track that leads to the cliffs (GPS: 29.144222, -13.505744). The fields here are good for the aforementioned birds, whilst the cliffs are a good place to search for the endemic flora.

Lanzarote Viper's-bugloss (top) and Brown Bluebell (bottom) two of many attractive wildflowers that grow near Haría.

With the car, follow the LZ-201 road in the direction *Mirador del Río*. The landscape remains attractive, with lots of places to explore for wildflowers.

Haría is the site for Canary on Lanzarote. Look and listen for it in the fields around the village.

After 5.6 kms from Haría, turn left to *Mirador del Río*. Follow this narrow road until there is a car park on the right.

6 Trom here you have gorgeous views over the island of La Graciosa and the desolate coastal plain at the foot of the cliffs (see cover photo). This is the most likely place to encounter Barbary Falcon and Ravens. From May-September, Eleonora´s Falcons fly by, and Egyptian Vulture and Osprey are also a possibility. The strategy for seeing these birds is patience – just admire the view and wait until they fly by. Botanists will enjoy Canary Rockrose and Pinnate Lavender at the edge of the cliffs.

7 The last stop is Mirador del Río, a fancy but stunning restaurant and viewpoint (entrance € 5,00). In terms of species there is no reason to go in but for the views and the building itself, it is worth it. The cliffs are at their steepest here and the view of La Graciosa is to die for. There are some very tame Berthelot's Pipits in the fields just before the viewpoint. The attractive Felty Sea Lavender* (*Limonium puberulum*) grows around here and we also found the desert butterfly Greenish Black-tip.

The view from Mirador del Río.

Route 5: La Corona

4 HOURS, 30 KM
EASY TO MODERATE

Impressive landscape of crater and lava fields.

Habitats: young lava field, succulent scrub, rocky coast
Selected species: Lanzarote Houseleek, Shrubby Madder, Balsam Spurge, Great Grey Shrike, Whimbrel, Atlantic Lizard, Eastern Canary Gecko, Canary Red Admiral, Jameos Blind Lobster* (*Munidopsis polymorpha*)

This route follows the lava flow of la Corona, an impressive volcano in the north of Lanzarote. It gives a wonderful chance to view several aspects of volcanism, including recent lava flows, the volcano crater, and lava caves. This is a laid-back route with beautiful landscapes and a fascinating insight in the volcanic history of the island – it is not the best route to see a lot of species.

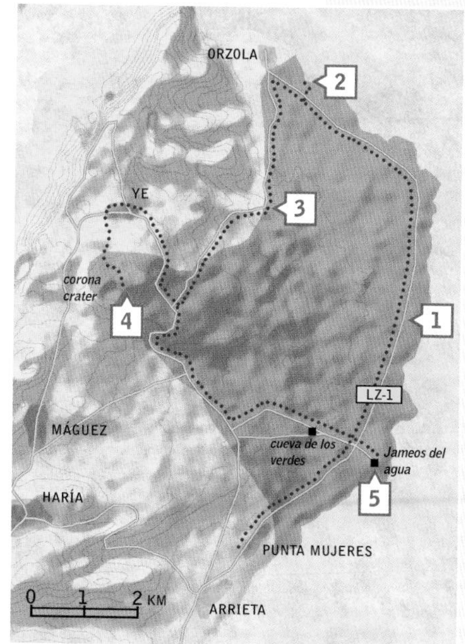

Starting point Punta Mujeres
Leave town in northern direction towards Orzola.

1 There are various places where you can park and enjoy the young lava fields of the *Malpaís de la Corona*. The entire field originates from a single eruption 3000 years ago which enlarged the island with 24 square km of lava. This is considered an old Malpaís as described on page 42. With all its cracks and clefts, it is a natural retreat for flora and fauna. The surreal landscape is home to many plants of the succulent scrub, such as Verode, King Juba's and Balsam Spurges and the Shrubby Madder, while the rocks are covered with many species of lichens.
Continue through the pitch-black lava field which, further ahead, is partially

overblown with white sand, creating a bizarre black-and-white landscape. Turn right towards the beach at km 32.

2 This beach is a pretty place to cool down and perhaps snorkel a bit. The lava fields here at the coast are dotted with wind-beaten, almost disk-shaped Balsam Spurges, plus some Zygophyllum bushes. Atlantic Lizards are very common. On the rocks, look for Whimbrel and other waders.

On entering Orzola village, turn left (Haría). Right after the sign that you are leaving Orzola, there is a track on your right (GPS: 29.202604, -13.451885). Park here.

3 The small trail into the lava field is worth a quick exploration. It is less exposed than the coastal lava fields and harbours more species.

Continue and at the crossing, turn right to the village of Ye. Park in the village at km 4 on the left side at the beginning of a track, just before the church (there is an option to park there too, if there is no space near the track).

The coast at point 2 with views of Órzola. A great point to go snorkelling

4 This is your chance to get up to a crater rim! Walk up the track. The first part leads through small fields surrounded by lichen-clad stone walls that protect the crops against the desiccating winds. Look for Trumpeter Finch here.

Close to the base of the crater, the route (now a trail) moves through lichen-clad rocks where some houseleeks and East Canary Sow-thistle* (*Sonchus pinnatifidus*) grow. The great attraction here is the crater rim itself. Look inside and imagine the immense force of the eruption that took place here. It produced a crater of 190 metre deep and 450 metre wide at its upper part.

Return to the car and follow the road back, now looking for the signs for *Cueva de los Verdes* and *Jameos del Agua*. You are now following the lava flow down to the sea.

5 The Cueva de los Verdes and Jameos del Agua are both part of an underground cave system 11 km in length from the Corona crater into the Atlantic. The tunnel was formed when the hot lava stream cooled. The outer ring cooled and solidified much quicker than the interior, which continued to flow for a while, leaving a hollow tube.
We advise to visit to the Jameos del Agua (€ 10,00 2023 prices). This is a segment of the lava tunnel that was filled with sea water. With it came a small lobster that, trapped in this confined area, evolved into a species of its own: the small, pale, blind cave-dwelling Munidopsis polymorpha. A superb example of evolution on islands, only this time the ecological 'island' is a cave!
Besides the lobster, which occurs by the thousands in the central part of the cave and is easily seen on the dark rocks, Jameos del Agua is a superb, laid-back and cool place, with hanging gardens, a wonderful bar and a good exhibition on the island's geology. It is designed by the famous Lanzarote artist César Manrique (see page 58). Canary Red Admiral frequents the beautiful flowers in the gardens of the Centre.

The beautiful Jameos del Agua is part of a lava tunnel. One of its great attractions is the small blind lobster Munidopsis polymorpha, which' entire population is restricted to this cave!

Route 6: La Graciosa

6 HOURS, 17 KM
EASY TO MODERATE

A visit to a pristine island.
Good birdwatching, especially sea birds between March to October.

Ferry crossing € 26,- return fair; Bicycle hire € 10,- per day

Habitats: cliffs, sandy desert and dunes, succulent scrub
Selected species: Traganum, Sea Spurge, *Polycarpaea nivea*, Common Dolphin, Hoopoe, Great Grey Shrike, Stone Curlew, Barbary Falcon, Eleonora's Falcon, Osprey, Cory's Shearwater, Red-billed Tropicbird, Atlantic Lizard, Lanzarote Greenish Blacktip

The small island of La Graciosa (meaning both 'the amusing' and 'the graceful' in Spanish) has only 700 inhabitants, divided between two small villages. The island measures 8 km in length and 4 km in width, and about 90% of its surface is covered with a (near)-natural vegetation of semi-desert and dunes. There is no place quite like it in the entire Canary Islands archipelago – at least no place you can visit, as the other islands of the Chinijo Archipelago are not accessible. All these islands, including La Graciosa and the sea between them, are part of a protected nature park.

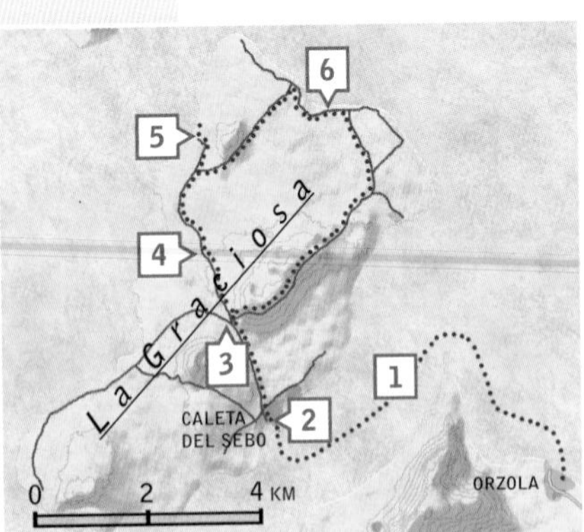

Starting point Orzola harbour
There are two ferry companies with departures every 1 to 2 hours: Lineas Romero (**www.lineasromero.com**) and Biosfera Express (**www.biosferaexpress.com.es**).

1 The crossing over the 2 km wide strait between Lanzarote and La Graciosa takes about 25 minutes and passes underneath the dramatic Famara cliffs. Birdwatching can be very rewarding, with Osprey, Barbary Falcon and Little Egret year-round and Cory's Shearwater (which

breeds in the cliffs) from late February to late October. Summer and autumn are the best, as you have a chance of seeing Bulwer's Petrel and even Red-billed Tropicbird. Common Dolphin is also sometimes seen.

The boat rounds the northern cape of the Famara cliffs (top). In season (April – October) it is a superb trip to spot sea birds. The most common species here is the Cory's Shearwater (bottom).

2 You can rent a bicycle in front of the dock of Caleta de Sebo (the village of La Graciosa) where you arrive. Follow the cycling route given on the map. Note that the track can be quite bumpy in places. Alternatively, you can walk it (beautiful, but very long) or by 4-wheel drive (with a driver but expensive).

Before you start, check the little harbour for waders, and the village for Hoopoes and Great Grey Shrikes. Of course, keep your eyes open all along the route, but especially at the following points.

3 The main junction lies on the ridge between the two main craters. There are a few allotments here with cactuses, which seem to attract birds. Look out for Hoopoe, Great Grey Shrike, Spectacled Warbler, Stone Curlew and Cattle Egret. We found the Greenish Black-tip here and elsewhere on the island.

4 Continue in the direction Las Conchas. You now pass through a magnificent, empty plain of original semi-desert vegetation. Some Houbara Bustards breed here (or elsewhere in suitable habitat on the island), but chances of seeing them are rather slim.

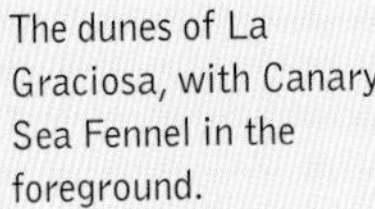

The dunes of La Graciosa, with Canary Sea Fennel in the foreground.

5 Follow the track to the pristine Las Conchas beach, which is found one third of the way along the circuit. From the beach you have splendid views of the uninhabited islands of Montaña Clara and La Alegranza. On these islands, a large proportion of the rare sea birds of the Canaries breed, but since they only come ashore at night, they are not frequently seen. The dunes here are attractive from a botanical point of view: Traganum, Canary Sea Fennel, Sea Spurge, Alfalfa Dodder, parasitising on Shrubby Launaea, and Warty Sea-lavender are just a few plants you'll find here. Atlantic Lizards (often rather big specimens here) are very common.

Continue the circuit, crossing another ridge between two craters. Beyond it, the landscape becomes sandier.

6 The track reaches the sea again, at another beach. The scatter of small, rounded stones here turns out to be, on closer inspection, the half-fossilized nests of Anthophora bees, a group of hairy bees that still occurs on the islands (see page 35). The strange Traganum bush is very common.

Continue the circuit back to the village.

Additional remarks You'll enjoy a visit to La Graciosa even more when you spend a night here, so you'll have an evening and morning to visit the plains in the north. The solitude is splendid then.

Additional sites on Lanzarote and Chinijo

See map on page 99 for the location of the following sites.

A – The Lanzarote-Fuerteventura ferry

Keep your eyes open on this 20 minute crossing. Cory´s Shearwater (March to October) can get very close to the boat and any of the local seabirds can be expected. Marine mammals such as Short-finned Pilot Whale, Common and Bottlenose Dolphins have been observed. Flying fish are frequently seen from the ferry.

Fagonia is a common wildflower that is often found growing in the dark lava pebbles (*lapilli*).

B – Playa Blanca

GPS: 28.855852, -13.872094 The tourist complex of Playa Blanca at the southern end of Lanzarote is a popular base for birdwatchers with a family. It is close to the Janubio saltpans (route 1) and there is some good birding within walking distance. The ornamental vegetation of the village can be good for migrant birds and Spanish Sparrow is common. The old lighthouse of Punta Pechiguera is a suitable site to do some seawatching. Early morning and late evening are the best time of the day. To the north and east there are desert plains with a rich bird life, but they are difficult to visit.

C – Playa Papagayo

GPS: 28.843499, -13.786643 This famous and beautiful beach is situated in a natural reserve. This is perhaps the best place on Lanzarote to do some snorkelling and discover the astonishing sea life. The entrance fee is 3 euro for a car. There are also taxi-boats from Playa Blanca.

D – El Golfo

GPS: 28.979725, -13.829295 El Golfo in Timanfaya National Park is a scenic oddity. It is a half-submerged volcano, a semicircular amphitheatre open to the ocean. When the hot lava hit the sea water during a massive eruption, no ash could be formed, and unstable rock appeared. The porous lava and erosion have created bizarre formations with a multitude of red and russet colours. The lake has an intense green colour, caused by green algae, and

The Famara cliffs

is linked with the ocean by a subterranean tunnel. El Golfo is signposted in Yaiza.

E – Walk along the Famara cliffs

GPS: 29.117825, -13.538960 There are two rough tracks along the west side of the Famara cliffs. The lower one runs close to beach and is popular among surfers (you can drive it). The upper one is longer and less travelled and forms a spectacular backdrop for a long hike. The superb landscape and, as you proceed, the quietude, is wonderful. Botanically, this is an interesting route (with the white-flowered gold-coin Asteriscus schultzii the star species), while the typical Famara cliff birds (Cory's Shearwater, Raven, Barbary Falcon and Osprey) are likely to cross overhead or through the strait.

The track starts behind the Urbanización Famara (see map on page 106). At the start, the track splits in an upper and lower section, but they reunite further ahead.

F – Presa de Mala

GPS 29.101018, -13.477702 The only freshwater reservoir on Lanzarote has been built near the village called Mala in the north-east. When wet, the spot attracts herons and waders, like Whimbrel and Black-winged Stilt. The track over leads through a hilly arid landscape which is good for Trumpeter Finch, Spectacled Warbler and Raven.

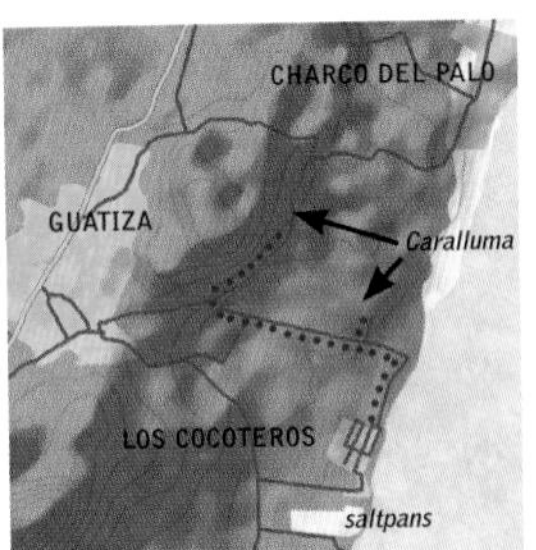

Presa de Mala is reached by turning off the LZ-1 to the village of Mala, and once in Mala, taking the first right, which leads further as a small country road that crosses the LZ-1 and continues as dirt track to the dam, which lies 2 km from the bridge.

G –Barranco Teneguime

GPS 29.076069, -13.490748. Another great walking route is the track up the Barranco Teneguime. The landscape is beautiful and it is a good place to find some interesting plants (e.g. Campylanthus), butterflies and other insects (e.g. Greenish Black-tip) and Eastern Canary Gecko. To arrive at the barranco, go to Guatiza. From the centre, take the Calle Álamo that crosses the bridge over the LZ-1. Immediately across it you can turn left on a dirt road to park. On foot, go back to the road and cross it, following the trail through the barranco underneath the slope.

The strange Caralluma is the star species of the Cocoteras lava fields. The finger-like stems blend in perfectly in the chaotic lava fields and are not easy to find (left).

H – Salt pans and lava fields of Cocoteras

GPS: 29.073017, -13.468823 and 29.061143, -13.460385 At the small saltpans, migrating waders may show up such as Little Stint, Curlew Sandpiper, Dunlin and Black-winged Stilt. The lava fields offer a fine walk and are a main site for the endemic Caralluma which flowers in winter. It grows on undisturbed rocky lava (not on the cultivated fields). Look for a squat square stemmed small cactus.
The salt pans are located just south of the tiny village of Cocoteras and east of Guatiza. The lava fields are to the north. We propose the route on the map.

I – Whale-watching from the eastern shore

GPS: 29.019537, -13.465298 If you want to spot whales and dolphins, the eastern shore provides excellent opportunities, but timing and location are key. It's best to visit on calm days with little wind and find a spot at a higher altitude overlooking the ocean. A great option is just north of Teguise, where you can follow a path to a small village called Los Ancones. From there, continue a bit further, either on foot or with caution in a car, and then turn right to reach the hilltop with a view of the ocean.
One of our readers shared this location with us and reported sightings of Risso's, Striped,

Bottlenose, and Common Dolphins, as well as Cuvier's Beaked Whale, Fin, Sei, and Bryde's Whale during the winter. It's an exciting variety, especially considering that this site is not widely known. Due to its relative obscurity, it's uncertain what can be seen during other times of the year. However, considering the elevation and the deep waters close to the shore, it's worth exploring this area.

J – Lanzarote Aquarium

GPS 29.003725, -13.487481 Lanzarote Aquarium has a large collection of fish from Canary Islands waters, such as the triggerfish, golden fishes and fulas. There are six so-called touching-pools where both children and adults can touch and enjoy animals such as sea cucumbers, starfish, sea urchins, coastal-zone fish and small crabs. The aquarium is located in Centro Comercial el Trébol, in Costa Teguise. It opens from 12 to 6 pm. Prices (in 2023) are € 15.- for adults and € 10.- for children. **www.aquariumlanzarote.com**

K – Seabird and whale watching on the Banco de la Concepción

Some 71 km out in the Atlantic lie the shallows of the Banco de la Concepción, an outstanding area in marine diversity. Here the ocean is “only” 170 to 200 metres deep and offers an attractive environment for a multitude of whales, dolphins, turtles, sharks, tuna and other fish. Lots of sea birds, including those that breed on the islands of the Chinijo archipelago, come here to feed. The importance of this area for seabirds, particularly rarities, has only recently been appreciated. Regular attractions include Wilson´s, Madeiran and White-faced Storm-petrels, Bulwer's Petrel and Barolo Shearwater plus a mouth-watering selection of rarities like Red-billed Tropicbird, Fea’s/Zino’s and Swinhoe’s Storm-petrels, Black-bellied Storm-petrel and South Polar Skua (one of five potential skuas present!) some of which may yet prove to be annual in small numbers. Up to nine species of cetaceans have also been seen.

Since 2010 two-day pelagic tours to the area have been organized in summer by Lanzarote pelagics whose website (**lanzarotepelagics.blogspot.co.uk**) is a valuable resource. However, at the time of writing, the company seems dormant, but it’s worth checking for any future trips.

Wilson's Storm-petrel is a summer visitor to the Banco de Concepción.

Fuerteventura

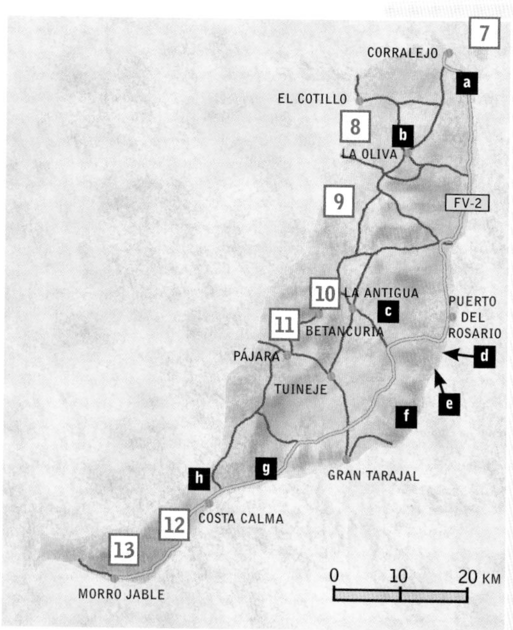

Although Fuerteventura is, like Lanzarote, a dry and fairly low island, it has a quite different character. If Lanzarote is the island of volcanoes, Fuerteventura is the island of deserts. There are fewer lava fields and volcanoes, but there are more desert plains. The sombre slaty-black of Lanzarote is replaced by terracotta soils (all of which are, of course, of volcanic origin).

Fuerteventura is twice the size of Lanzarote, and the second largest of the Canary Islands (only Tenerife is larger). Fuerteventura has fewer inhabitants than Lanzarote, though, and mass tourism is largely confined to coastal sites like Corralejo, Caleta de Fuste, Gran Tarajal, Cotillo, Costa Calma and Morro Jable. Further inland, the villages of La Oliva, Antigua, Tuineje and Betancuria have retained much of their original character.

Fuerteventura has a mixture of rocky hills and extensive plains. The three main ranges are Bentancuria in the west (route 10 and 11), Cuchillos de Vigán in the east (page 149) and the highest range in the south: La Jandía, with its spectacular cliffs (route 12 and 13). Life concentrates in the valleys and barrancos (routes 10, 11), but many of the desert birds are found on the plains (route 8 and 9).

These desert plains run down from the north shore near Corralejo south to La Oliva (route 8) and then through the eastern and western mountain ranges further south to Gran Tarajal. Near Corralejo (site B on page 147) and on the isthmus connecting La Jandía with the rest of Fuerteventura (route 12 and site I on page 150), there are extensive areas of sand dunes, which again support a different wildlife.

Note that on none of the routes, you'll find much shade. When doing the walks in this book, make sure you have protection against the sun (including sunglasses) and sufficient water with you.

Route 7: Isla de Lobos

FULL DAY
EASY

Easy and beautiful walk over a pristine island.
Superb snorkelling.

Habitats: open sea, dunes, lagoons, malpaìs, salt marsh
Selected species: Barolo Shearwater, Cory's Shearwayer, Black-winged Stilt, migrating waders, Balsam Spurge, the sea lavenders *Limonium bollei* and *Limonium tuberculatum*, Zygophyllum, Parrot Fish

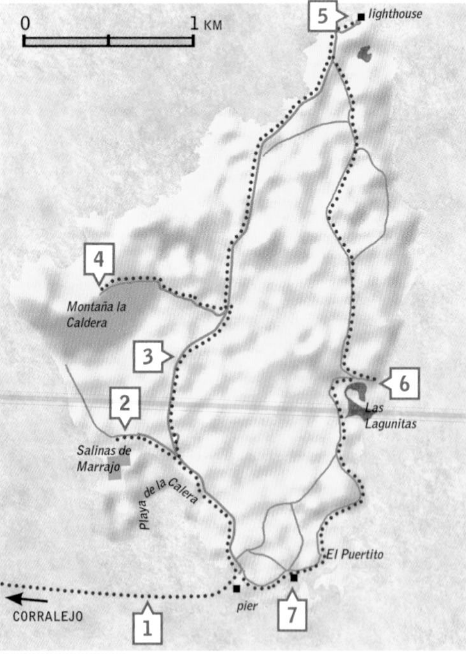

The island of Lobos and its surrounding marine habitats have been a protected reserve since 1982, making it one of the first natural parks of the Canary Islands. The island has a surprising botanical diversity with over 130 species plants, including the endemic *Limonium bollei*, a beautiful sea lavender. Furthermore, it hosts a great variety of seabirds, including the rare Barolo Shearwater and several species of storm petrel. Finally, its surrounding crystal-clear shallow waters are an important area for sea life, making it an ideal place to go snorkelling. Important notice – make sure you bring food and water with you on the trip.

Starting point Corralejo harbour. There are several companies offering ferries to the Isla de Lobos, and tickets can be arranged online or on the spot. Note that a permit is required to visit the island. You can obtain it yourself via www.lobospass.com or have your ferry company to arrange it for a small price. You have the choice between a regular boat and one with a glass bottom. The latter is more expensive but adds another experience –views of the sea bottom. On a glass-bottom boat you notice how shallow the strait between Fuerteventura and Isla de Lobos actually is! Unfortunately, the sea floor slides away under the boat too fast to recognise any sea life.

The spring-flowering sea-lavender *Limonium tuberculatum* is restricted to Los Lobos and the south of Gran Canaria. Outside the Canaries it is found on the Cape Verde Islands and coastal Morocco.

1 The boat trip offers an excellent opportunity for close views of seabirds. Cory's Shearwater is plentiful, and anything else might show up, including, with luck, Barolo Shearwater. Once on Los Lobos, walk down the pier and turn left towards Playa de la Calera. Follow the main path and eventually, turn left at the big sign about the Salinas del Marrajo.

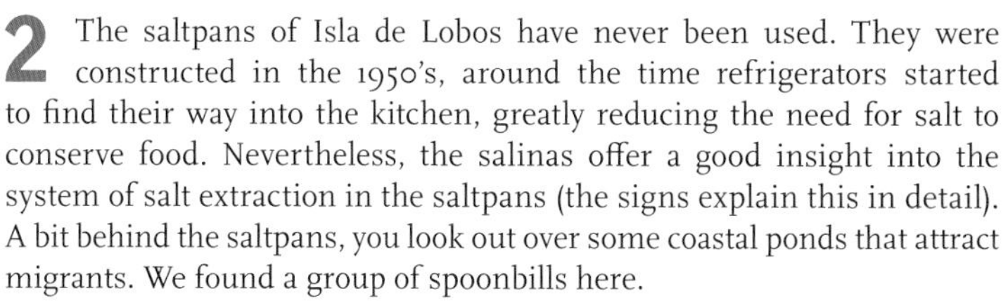

2 The saltpans of Isla de Lobos have never been used. They were constructed in the 1950's, around the time refrigerators started to find their way into the kitchen, greatly reducing the need for salt to conserve food. Nevertheless, the salinas offer a good insight into the system of salt extraction in the saltpans (the signs explain this in detail). A bit behind the saltpans, you look out over some coastal ponds that attract migrants. We found a group of spoonbills here.

Return the way you came and continue along the main path.

3 The path alternately runs through *malpaís* and dunes, where the shrubby sea lavender *Limonium tuberculatum* is the most striking plant. In the malpaís, Balsam Spurge is particularly common, with some truly impressive and old individuals.

At the next junction, turn left towards the Montaña la Caldera and ascend it.

4 From the caldera, you can enjoy a wonderful view over the island and its position in the strait between Fuerteventura and Lanzarote. The sea-facing side of the mountain is where many of the rare sea birds of the Canary Islands breed, although chances of seeing them here are slim as they typically only come to shore at night.

The saline lagoon of Las Lagunitas has a rich flora and often attracts waders.

Find your way back down and continue the trail towards the lighthouse.

5 The faro was built in 1865 and the lighthouse keeper was, for a long time, the only inhabitant of the island. By now, the lighthouse is automatic and there is no need for a permanent lighthouse keeper, meaning that the island is officially uninhabited. The pond near the lighthouse is an excellent place to look for Black-winged Stilts and during migration and in winter, other waders that might show up. Don't forget to take a look over sea for sea birds. Cory's shearwater is often present, and who knows what more might show up!

Turn back and turn left towards Las Lagunitas.

6 Las Lagunitas is perhaps the most special part of the island. It has a rich flora that even includes its own endemic sea lavender, *Limonium bollei*, which is sometimes called the Lobos Houseleek, an ill-chosen name as it is not even remotely related to the houseleeks. Las Lagunitas is another great place to look for migrating waders.

Continue and turn left on the next crossing towards El Puertito.

7 El Puertito (the little harbour) is near the spot the ferry docks and forms an excellent place to spend the remainder of your time on the island, snorkelling. The sheltered bay with its gradual slopes allows for easy access, while the secluded position limits the size of the waves. A wide diversity of species can be found here. The iconic Parrot Fish can be particularly common here.

Route 8: The Tindaya plains

FULL DAY
60 KM

Best place for steppe and desert birds on Fuerteventura.
Superb plains with red soils, dark lava and white sands.

Habitats: rocky plains, sandy plains, fields, malpaís, barrancos, rocky coast
Selected species: Kleinia, King Juba's Spurge, Barbary Ground Squirrel, Egyptian Vulture, Buzzard, Houbara Bustard, Cream-coloured Courser, Eastern Canary Gecko

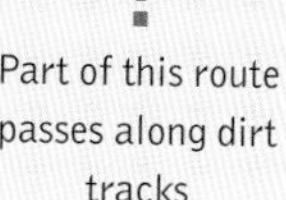

Part of this route passes along dirt tracks

This car route covers a combination of wide and windy stony plains, small fields and an expanse of white sand dunes with the nearby shore and sea. The plains are about the best on Fuerteventura for steppe birds, while the fields and gardens of La Oliva are excellent for birds of agricultural land. Indeed, birds are the great draw of this route, but the stunning open landscape, the variety of habitats and the ample opportunities to step out and explore, make it an attraction for every kind of naturalist. Keep in mind though, that to see the steppe birds, it is best to explore these sites at dawn or towards dusk.

At the time of writing, the tracks were generally good to navigate but a little rough in some places.

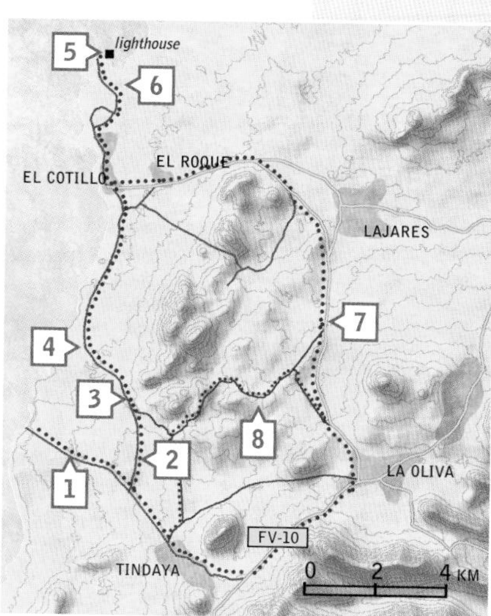

Starting point Tindaya (on the FV-10). Cross the village and (carefully) follow the potholed road to the coast that starts from the village's west end.

1 Drive slowly and stop on high vantage points to scan for steppe birds. Houbara Bustard is frequently seen here, while Cream-coloured Courser, Stone-Curlew and Black-bellied Sandgrouse can be present as well. The most common birds here are Lesser Short-toed Lark and, of course, Berthelot's Pipit. In the shrubby places, look for Spectacled

The Tindaya plains support some of the highest numbers of Houbara and Cream-colored Courser on Fuerteventura.

Warbler, while small flocks of Trumpeter Finch, and, more rarely, Linnet, roam the plains. We urge you to stay on the track in order not to disturb the fragile bird life. It is best to stay in the car and use it as a hide.

Return and follow the (only) track to the left (north; GPS: 28.606301, -14.002336).

2 The track passes more excellent semi-desert with all the aforementioned birds possible.

3 The track enters a barranco. Turn left and follow the gully until the track reappears on the other side (GPS: 28.630662, -14.005479). Note that this section may have some tricky spots. If you can't cross, retrace your steps to Tindaya and drive around to pick up the route from Cotillo on the other side. The barranco itself is a pretty place, lined with large Canary Tamarisks.

4 The track leaves the barranco and continues towards El Cotillo. The steppe plain here is again excellent habitat for all steppe birds early in the morning (during the day, the track along the coast becomes busy).

Cross Cotillo, a rather unattractive modern settlement, following the direction of the lighthouse (*Faro de Tostón*).

5 The lighthouse area offers good views over the coastline and the ocean. Seawatching with a telescope may produce high numbers of Cory´s Shearwater, especially in the evenings from March to September. Explore the area around the lighthouse on foot. The many tidal pools on the shore support a good variety of wintering and migrating waders, and usually hold some Little Egrets. Warty Sea-lavender* (*Limonium pappillatum*) grows close to the road.

6 The dunes just before the lighthouse are worth exploring as well. Sea-heath, Canary Sea Fennel (*Astydamia latifolia*) and

Narrow-leaved Restharrow* (*Ononis angustissima*) are common wildflowers, while Barbary Partridge, Hoopoe, Stone Curlew, Trumpeter Finch and even Houbara may turn up.

Return to Cotillo and take the FV-10 to La Oliva. Continue for 10 kms (passing the town of Lagares), the road crosses a lava field. Over the hill, just beyond a white building, turn left onto a section of the old road. Park here (GPS: 28.643023, -13.945490).

7 Explore the malpaís. Verode and King Juba's Spurge are the common succulent plants, while the rare Burchard's Caralluma has been found here too (although it is easier to find at another part of the Malpaís described at site B on page 147). Barbary Ground Squirrel, Trumpeter Finch and Barbary Partridge are all present in the lava field, while underneath suitable flat stones, Eastern Canary Gecko can be frequent.

Continue and at the entrance sign of La Oliva, turn a sharp right (GPS: 28.623349, -13.942233).

8 This track leads again through a good area for Houbara Bustard. The best time is in the late afternoon, when small groups gather. Cream-coloured Courser may also be seen.
If you're feeling adventurous, you can continue this track, driving along a fence and eventually turning left on a T-junction after 7.2 km (GPS: 28.616690, -13.988893) to find your way back to Tindaya. Otherwise, turn around and drive back via the main road.

Female (right) and male (left) of the Fuerteventura Stonechat. This bird is frequent in the barrancos of this route.

Route 9: Los Molinos reservoir

3-4 HOURS
16 KM

One of the best birding sites on Fuerteventura

Habitats: freshwater reservoir, ravines, desert plains
Selected species: Fuerteventura Stonechat, Black-bellied Sandgrouse, Houbara Bustard, Cream-coloured Courser, Trumpeter Finch, Ruddy Shelduck, Black-winged Stilt

Los Molinos reservoir is famous among birdwatchers. It is the only permanent freshwater body of any size on the island, hence a major draw for birds, such as ducks, herons and waders. Moreover, it is set in a stony plateau where all of Fuerteventura's steppe bird species are present and frequently show as well.
The trip to Los Molinos is clearly a route for birdwatchers, but since all the action is concentrated on a small area, with some interesting walking options nearby and an open-air museum, it is good too for naturalists with wider interests.

Starting point Tefia

Drive south and at the first junction turn right to las Parcelas.

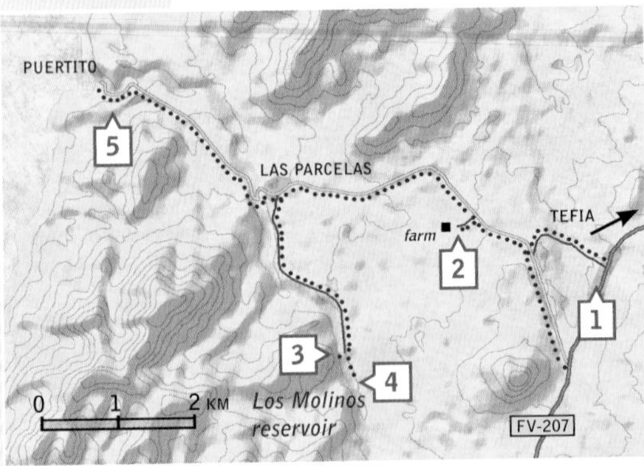

1 Just before this junction lies the open air *Ecomuseo La Alcogida*. Houses and a windmill of this abandoned settlement have been beautifully restored and now offer an insight into the former rural life of Fuerteventura.

Follow the road to Las Parcelas. Between km 2 and 3, turn left onto a track towards a goat farm (GPS: 28.527973, -14.013761).

2 The 50 metres of dirt track towards this farm offer good opportunities to scan the surrounding stony fields. Lesser Short-toed Larks are usually not far away, and we've seen Houbara Bustard and Cream-coloured Courser on various occasions. Note that here, as elsewhere, the plains seem deserted at first glance. You need to scan patiently, preferably with telescope, to find the birds.

Continue to Las Parcelas and in the bend after the 'soccer field' (a square of volcanic gravel with two sets of goal posts), turn left, signposted 'Presa de Molinos' (GPS: 28.530444, -14.040944). Continue until you reach the Los Molinos dam. The stretch towards the dam can be good for the desert birds mentioned on point 2 as well.
Park at the dam.

3 From the dam, scan the reservoir where Coot, Moorhen, Ruddy Shelduck and other ducks are present. On the banks of the reservoir, all kinds of waders can be found, such as Common Sandpiper, Greenshank, Black-winged Stilt and Little Ringed Plover. On the far side, in the ravine, there are usually Fuerteventura Stonechats while the abandoned shed by which you parked houses a colony of Spanish Sparrows.

4 For better views of the shorebirds, go to the western inlet of the lake. To do so, you'll have to cross the fence and walk the trail that runs along the reservoir. The gate is sometimes closed, but this is a public trail so you are allowed to continue.

Trumpeter Finch is frequent around the Los Molinos reservoir.

Return to Las Parcelas and turn left towards the coast.

5 In the secluded bay is a bar where you can enjoy some refreshments. At the entrance of the village, you'll encounter freshwater ponds that attract water birds and waders. A walking trail starts in the steep barranco, but it is closed in the breeding season. Fuerteventura Stonechat and Great Grey Shrike can be found here.

Route 10: Betancuria

!
No shade
Take precautions

3-4 HOURS
MODERATE

Fuerteventura's most beautiful village.
Lovely walk with an interesting flora and butterflies.

Habitats: urban park, fields, succulent scrub
Selected species: Fuerteventura Nauplius, Burchard's Caralluma, Fagonia, Buzzard, African Blue Tit, Sardinian Warbler, Monarch, Greenish Blacktip, Fuerteventura Green-striped White, Canary Red Admiral

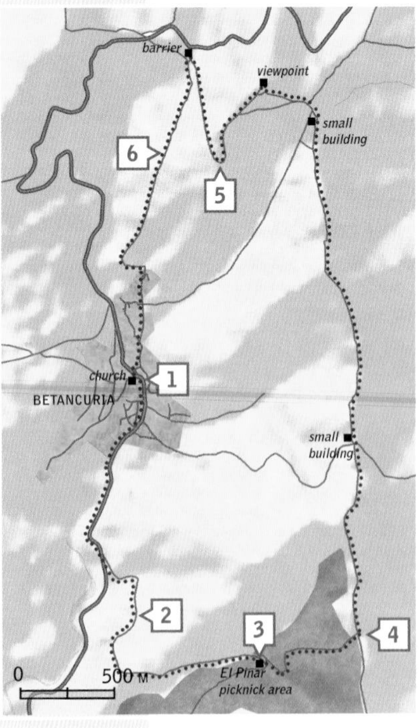

Betancuria is the oldest settlement of Fuerteventura and it shows its history clearly: the old church and surrounding houses are beautifully restored, and the whole village is set in a lovely landscape
The walk described here leads to a viewpoint with breath-taking vistas over the northern and eastern part of the island. The flora and butterfly fauna are rich (by Fuerteventuran standards) in and around the village and again at the peak.

Starting point Betancuria church

1 From the church, walk to the main road and go right (south). The park on your right is perhaps the best spot on the island to see the magnificent Monarch Butterfly, which flies around the treetops and comes down to drink the nectar of the planted Decaisne's Viper's-Bugloss. It is also a good place to track down the African Blue Tit, Sardinian Warbler and, in winter, Chiffchaff.

Continue down the main road, leaving the village. After about 800m, walk up a track to the left, signposted towards *Área recreativa Castillo de Lara.*

2 The track turns left at a small building, after which you'll walk through denser scrubland, with Shrubby Launaea, King Juba's Spurge and Balsam Spurge. The real highlight here is the strange Burchard's Caralluma, that is especially common under the shrubs and trees on the left side of the road. Also keep an eye open for Barbary Partridge and Great Grey Shrike that can occasionally be found here.

Continue until you reach the picknick area.

3 The picknick area of El Pinar is surrounded by higher pine trees, a strange sight for Fuerteventura. The area itself is a good place to look for birds, such as the African Blue Tit and Berthelot's Pipit.

Historic Betancuria (top) one of the best places on Fuerteventura to see Monarchs (bottom), here on the endemic (but planted) Decaisne's Viper's-bugloss.

Cross the picnic area and follow the trail further up.

4 At the ridge, you have superb views over the eastern part of the island, in particular the northern part of the Cuchillos de Vigán – a series of sharp, eroded mountain ranges (see page 149). On the slope, the big purple flower heads of Wild Artichoke (spring-summer) attract many insects. The endemic butterfly Greenish Black-tip can be frequent.

Continue to the left, following the ridge until you reach a small building (GPS: 28.422429, -14.045312). Here you can choose to either turn left

towards Betancuria, or continue your way along the ridge. Here we describe the latter option.
Follow the track along the ridge, past another small construction, up to the conspicuous viewpoint. From here, walk the tarmac road round the bend to the barrier.

5 This part is attractive for its wildflowers, and sometimes for insects as well. Both Canary Rockrose* (*Helianthemum canariense*) and Thyme-leaved Rockrose (*H. thymiphyllum*; endemic to the eastern islands) flowers here, as does Fagonia, Bonnet's Viper's-bugloss (*Echium bonnetii*), Pastor's Asparagus* (*Asparagus pastorianus*) and a few Fuerteventura Gold-coin* (*Asteriscus sericeus*). There are also some bushes of the Australian Cyclops Acacia.

Just before the barrier, follow the GR 131 trail to the left back to Betancuria.

6 In winter and spring, the fields show a colourful display of wildflowers, mainly Reichardia, Bonnet's Viper's-bugloss, Canary Rockrose, Lanzarote Bird's-foot-trefoil and Fagonia. Look carefully for butterflies, which include Clouded Yellow, Common Blue, Fuerteventura Green-striped White and Canary Red Admiral.

The path follows the ridge in the Betancuria mountains (bottom). Along the way, there are many attractive species, such as Thyme-leaved Rockrose (left) and Fuerteventura Green-striped White (right).

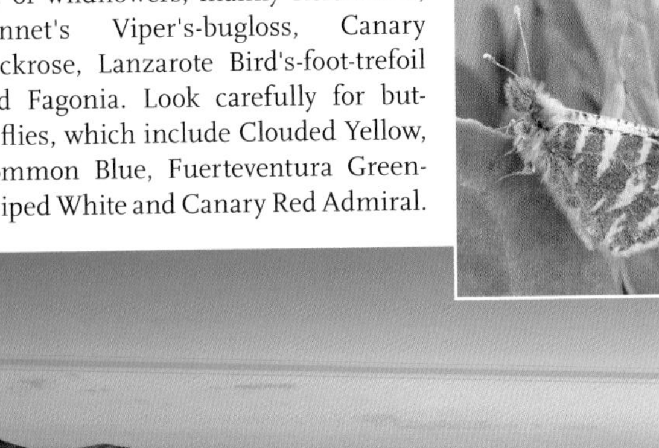

Route 11: Vega de Río Palma

4 HOURS, 24 KM
EASY - MODERATE

Reservoir and barranco which attract a rich birdlife and butterfly fauna.
A landscape that looks like a postcard of an oasis in the Sahara Desert.

Habitats: barranco, tamarisk scrub, village gardens, fields, succulent scrub
Selected species: Canary Palm Tree, Fuerteventura Nauplius, Balsam Spurge, King Juba's Spurge, Barbary Ground Squirrel, Raven, Buzzard, Barbary Partridge, African Blue Tit, Canary Island Chat, East Canary Gecko, East Canary Skink, Epaulet Skimmer

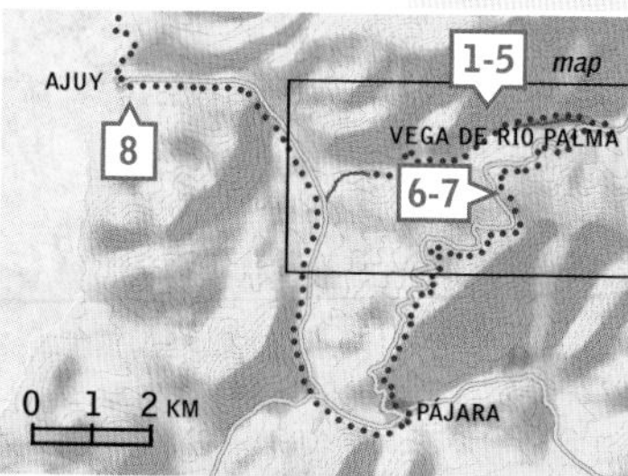

In the Betancuria mountains, situated in the arid red soils, lies the small village of Vega de Río Palma. Windmills pump up water for irrigation, making this a relatively green area. Like a true oasis, the village is surrounded by native Canary Date Palms, tamarisk thickets and cultivations. This route combines a scenic walk with some nearby stops to be visited by car. The relative

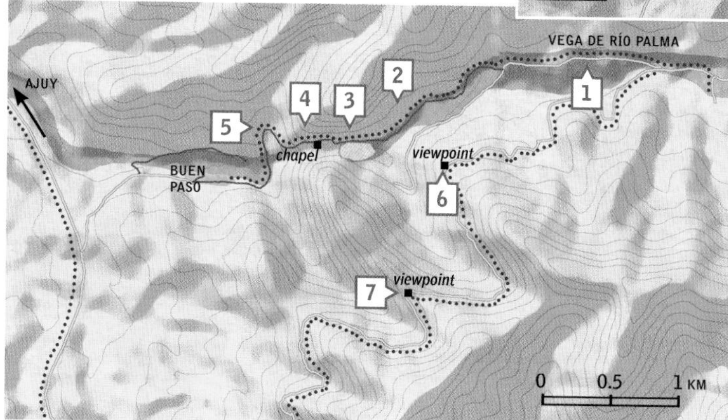

The oasis of Vega de Río Palma, seen from the small reservoir. The reservoir is now silted up and usually dry, but the surrounding tamarisk thickets are still a magnet to African Blue Tit, Sardinian Warbler and many migrants.

abundance of water makes this route attractive not only for finding small birds, but also for wildflowers, butterflies, dragonflies and reptiles.

Starting point Church of Vega de Río Palma

Follow the main street in south-western direction (direction Pájara) and turn right onto a small tarmac road, signposted again Vega de Río Palma.

1 In the village gardens, search for Sardinian Warbler, Greenfinch (rare on the island) and African Blue Tit. Keep an eye out too for butterflies (e.g. Greenish Black-tip, Fuerteventura Green-striped White and Clouded Yellow).

2 At the bridge (GPS: 28.393698, -14.087692), follow the trail along the dry riverbed to the former reservoir. Succulent bushes of Verode and King Juba's Spurge are common. Look underneath stones for reptiles. This is one of the very few places where the Eastern Canary Skink occurs. It hides under rocks and so is very hard to find.

3 Before reaching the reservoir, you pass through thickets of Canary Tamarisk, where both African Blue Tit and Sardinian Warbler are common. Migrant birds are also attracted to the lush vegetation, so at the right time, be prepared to find warblers, buntings, Bee-eaters or other birds. The reservoir itself is now dry. It silted up and will not be dug out, much to the disapproval of the local farming community. It is unclear to what extent this has affected the local dragonfly community (there are temporary puddles of standing water in the gorge), but this used to be the hotspot for dragonflies on Fuerteventura, supporting Sahara Bluetail, Epaulet Skimmer, Broad Scarlet and Blue Emperor.

4 Beyond the dam the landscape changes dramatically as you enter a narrow gorge that leads towards a small chapel.

5 As you leave the gorge, the trail bends to the right and enters a wider gorge. This is again a very good site for birds. Fuerteventura Stonechat is relatively common, while the rocky slopes are one of the best places to find Barbary Partridge on the island. Look out for Linnet, Trumpeter Finch, Raven, Buzzard and (less frequently) Egyptian Vulture.

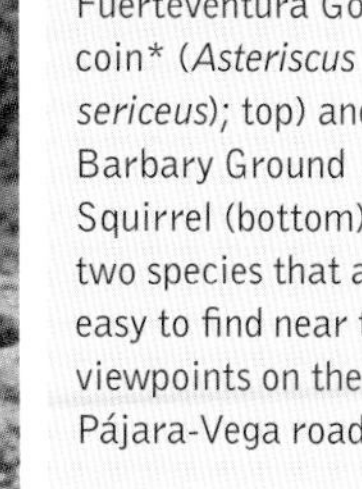

Fuerteventura Goldcoin* (*Asteriscus sericeus*); top) and Barbary Ground Squirrel (bottom) – two species that are easy to find near the viewpoints on the Pájara-Vega road.

African Blue Tit breeds in the tall vegetation of Vega de Río Palma.

Continue to the village of Buen Paso ahead where the arid fields may host more birds.

Return to Vega de Río Palma by the same way.

Take the car and drive in the direction of Pájara. There are two viewpoints along the way, both worth a stop.

6 The first one (GPS: 28.386970, -14.092385) has scenic views over the valley of Vega de Río Palma. You'll probably see some tame Barbary Ground Squirrels as well, which come to beg for peanuts. Botanists may want to walk along the road to look at the flashy Fuerteventura Gold-coin* (*Anteriscus sericeus*) on the hill slopes.

7 The second has a larger car park a little off the road (GPS: 28.379187, -14.094878). Here are usually some tame Ravens about. Note how much smaller this local race, isolated for many millennia, is than the European Ravens, and note too their different call and brownish necks. Barbary Ground Squirrels are present too and very tame and easy to photograph.

Continue towards Pájara, an attractive village, inviting you to have a drink. From here, go on to Ajuy and leave your car at the entrance of this little village.

8 From the beach of Ajuy, a 1 km trail goes up the rocky coast. It leads through white fossil dunes and ends near some caves eroded by the waves. It is a photogenic spot. The area of Ajuy is geologically the oldest part of the Canary Islands. Fossils have been found of molluscs and of an extinct shearwater species, *Puffinus holei*. Ajuy is where Jean de Béthencourt landed in 1402 to claim Fuerteventura for Castile.

Route 12: La Jandía

FULL DAY
96 KM

Good birdwatching, especially during migration.
Some of the most impressive, barren landscapes of the island.
Home to the endemic, cactus-like Jandía Spurge.

Habitats: Sand dunes, salt marsh, cliffs, succulent scrub, urban park, volcanic semi-desert, sandy desert, rocky coast
Selected species: Jandía Spurge, Opophytum, Cistanche, Yellow Restharrow, Canary Spurge, Algerian Hedgehog, Spectacled Warbler, Cattle Egret, Monk Parakeet, Hadada Ibis, Sacred Ibis, Trumpeter Finch, Cory's Shearwater, Fuerteventura Stonechat, migrant waders and passerines

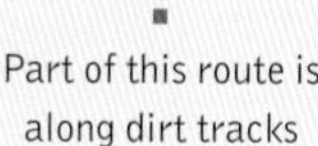

Part of this route is along dirt tracks

This may well be the most scenic route of Fuerteventura. The bare hills are part of the 2670 hectare large Jandía Nature Park. Botanically, this is Fuerteventura's treasure trove, but to find the best plants you need to explore the north-facing high cliffs (see next route).
This route's major attraction is the beautiful, if stern, landscape of this part of Fuerteventura – which, due to its southern and south-facing position, is

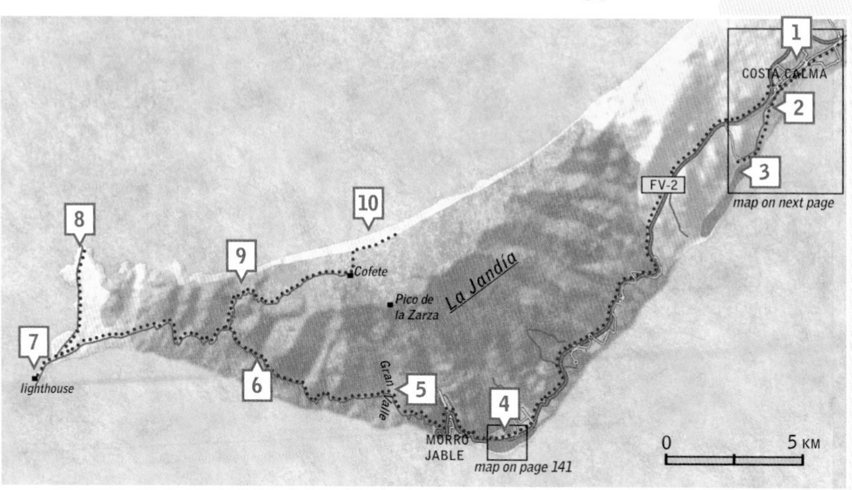

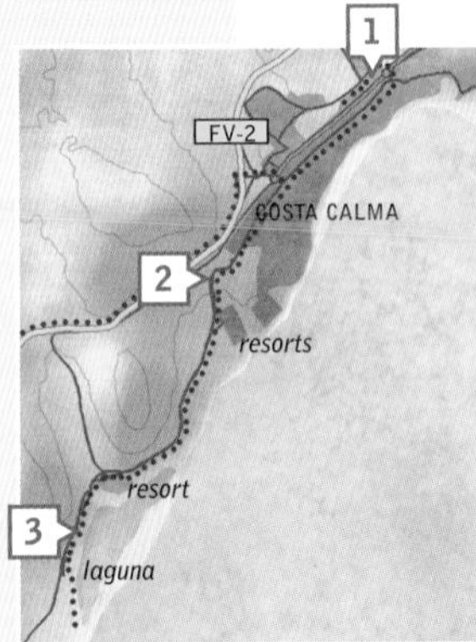

always a little hotter and more unforgiving than the rest of the desert island.

This route is designed as a car route with various walks, each of which you can make as long as you like. The west tip of Fuerteventura is a popular tourist outing. We advise to beat the crowds and leave early.

Starting point Costa Calma

1 The main road through the Costa Calma resort is bordered on either side by parks with palms and Casuarina Tree (superficially looking like a pine tree). The green oasis attracts migrant and wintering songbirds. Park at the large open area at the eastern roundabout and enter the park from here. Hoopoe and Goldfinch are resident, while Chiffchaff and Blackcap winter. In the evening this is a good spot to look for Algerian Hedgehogs and Eastern Canary Geckos.

Cross the roundabout and then turn right, driving parallel to the main street. Outside town, the road becomes a dirt road to a couple of hotels. Before the first hotel, park at the large bend to the left (GPS: 28.152275, -14.237263).

2 Wander around in search of the parasitic Yellow Cis-tanche, which is particularly common along the main road to Morro Jable. Other plants and insects of sandy dunes may be present too.

Continue to a large seaside hotel surrounded by palm trees. Below the hotel lies an extensive sandy beach with a large lagoon with salt marsh. Walk along the lagoon (GPS: 28.135059, -14.247406).

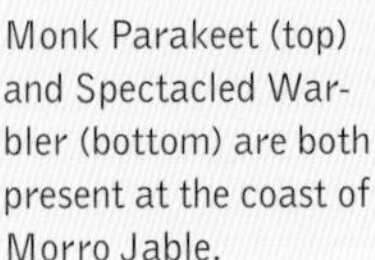

Monk Parakeet (top) and Spectacled Warbler (bottom) are both present at the coast of Morro Jable.

The prickly, cactus-like Jandía Spurge is endemic to the Jandía Peninsula, where it grows in just a few very dry, south-facing barrancos.

3 There are many shorebirds, such as Whimbrel, Sanderling and other waders, especially during migration. Little Egrets are often around and rare vagrant birds may turn up. Sadly, kite surfers are a great disturbance here.

Return to Costa Calma and take the FV-2 to Morro Jable.
In Moro Jable, park near the roundabout close to the lighthouse (conspicuous on your left) and walk the small circuit on the map.

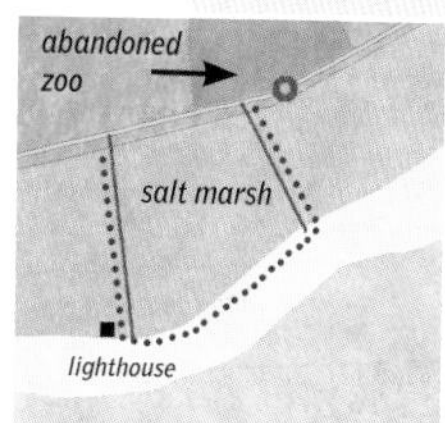

4 The coastal marshes around the lighthouse that can be a true gem. Spectacled Warbler, Cattle Egret and Great Grey Shrike are common, while in spring and autumn, as the marshes fill up after high tides, there can be many waders around. Check the palm trees along the abandoned zoo, where noisy feral Monk Parakeets and a small population of feral Sacred and Hadada Ibis reside (the latter two also in the palm trees).

Continue along the coast beyond Moro Jable.

5 The first stop on this track is the wide Gran Valle, from which a walking trail leads all the way to the hamlet of Cofete on the other side (this car route goes around the mountain and ends at Cofete). The

Gran Valle is home to Buzzard, while at the goat farm not far from the track, Trumpeter Finch is often about.

6 Two km before arriving at the turn to Cofete (GPS: 28.074337, -14.424424) you arrive at a broad barranco. walk up the dirt track into the valley. This is home to the botanical highlight of Fuerteventura, the cactus-like Jandía Spurge – a plant that only grows in the westernmost valleys of the Jandía peninsula, and only in the south facing ones, and no higher than 150 metres above sea level. There are few species worldwide with such a small and particular distribution!

Continue towards the lighthouse.

7 Before arriving at the little lighthouse, you cross a wide, deserted plain. Scenically, this is a superb area. It is home to a wide range of desert birds (e.g. Black-bellied Sandgrouse and Stone Curlew), but densities are very low, as are your chances of finding them here. From the lighthouse, you may see some Cory's Shearwaters and dolphins.

8 You can walk the coastal path from here to the Punta Pesebre or take the wide track to the headland by car. Look along the coast for the odd yellowish blobs of Opophytum,

Sacred Ibis breed in the abandoned zoo of Morro Jable.

The Canary Spurge, common on the western islands, is remarkably rare on Fuerteventura. There are some pretty specimens on the north side of La Jandía.

The empty plain of Cofete on the north side of La Jandía is the end goal of this route.

a succulent plant related to the ice plants. It is a frequent plant on the African coast, but on the Canaries, restricted to the tip of Jandía.
As most visitors only drive up to the lighthouse, you may have the Punta de Pesebre – yet another scenic highlight – all to yourself. This is a very desolate place, which overlooks a part of La Jandía's north coast that few people visit. This must be the view of Fuerteventura that Jean de Béthencourt enjoyed when he first set foot on the island (see history section).

Return and turn left to Cofete.

9 At the pass you have again beautiful views of the beach of Cofete. A little further on, the track passes along some impressive specimens of Canary Spurge, a rare plant on the eastern islands.

10 You can continue all the way to the beach of Cofete to enjoy a refreshing walk. This pristine beach is the only place in Europe where the massive Leatherback Turtle once laid its eggs (if one can call the Canary Islands a part of Europe). In a reintroduction program, young Leatherbacks were released here, and it is hoped that in a few decades, when they have matured, they will return to lay their eggs once more on Fuerteventura.

Route 13: Pico de la Zarza

FULL DAY, 8 KM (ONE WAY)
MODERATE-STRENUOUS

One of the most impressive walking routes on the island. Rare flora and superb views over La Jandia.

Habitat: Salt marsh, urban park, cliffs, rock desert, thermophilus scrubland
Selected species: Winter's Marguerite, Canary Aizoon, Jandia Viper's-bugloss, Raven, Fuerteventura Stonechat, migrant waders and passerines

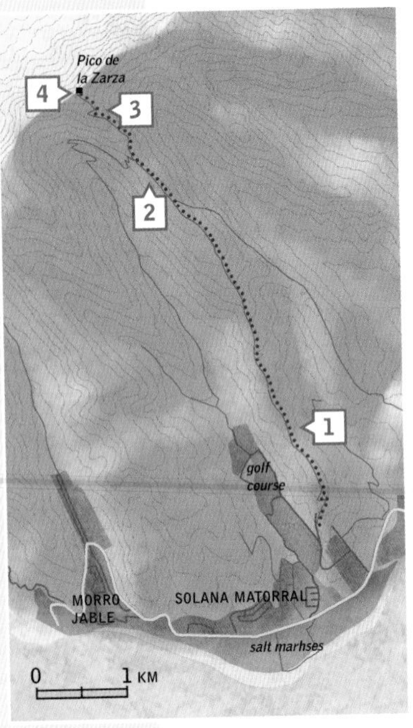

La Jandía is both the hottest and driest place of Fuerteventura, as well as the only area with some remnants of the moist forest vegetation that is found on the western islands. There is no forest here, but some shrubs that are home to these forests are present. This is the result of the high ridge catching the clouds.

This walk leads up to this ridge at its highest point: the 812m high Pico de la Zarza (also the highest point of the eastern islands). Along the track, you'll move from coastal salt marshes, through rocky deserts towards the shrubby ridge, where nurtured by clouds, a unique flora can be found.

Although the route follows an excellent track, the long uphill hike can be strenuous. The south slope completely lacks shade so it can be scorchingly hot. At higher elevations, clouds, rain and strong wind can also make it very cold. Try to pick a good day and leave early, pack enough water and food and use sunscreen – there is absolutely no shade to be found.

Starting point Car park at the beginning of the trail. (GPS: 28.059748, -14.328482).

Getting there from the second roundabout on the eastern part of Moro Jable turn off toward Vinamar and the golf course. Take the first left (golf

course again) go round the bend and then take the upper route to the car park near a white building.

Follow the trail from here.

1 The first, large section of the route is nearly barren, except for the occasional Shrubby Launaea. This plant is able to withstand the blistering heat that ravages these lower reaches of La Jandia. Its thorny appearance is not just for show: having no leaves limits evaporation and simultaneously protects against herbivores. In terms of birdlife, it is rather quiet, but keep an eye out for Barbary Falcon and Egyptian Vulture, which occasionally pass by.

2 About 3 km before the top, you will notice the first, welcome changes to the landscape. Most notably, the Shrubby Launaea is joined by more species such as Verode and King's Juba Spurge. In addition, you'll notice that lichens are growing on the rocks, indicating an increase in moisture. This is the result of frequent fog, a phenomenon that is known as

View of the Cofete plain from Pico de la Zarza (top). The cliffs support a fantastic flora. One species that grows in this are is Bonnet's Viper's-bugloss (bottom).

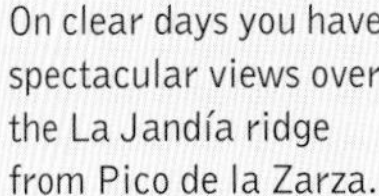

On clear days you have spectacular views over the La Jandía ridge from Pico de la Zarza.

horizontal precipitation (*llúvia horizontal*). Along the track Fuerteventura Stonechat is common.

3 Just as you pass the sign 1 km to the top, the vegetation drastically changes again. Winter's Marguerite* (*Argyranthemum winteri*) suddenly appears on the slopes in large numbers. In addition, with some careful searching, you might find small plants such as Canary Aizoon.

4 Of all the breathtaking views that Fuerteventura offers, the one from its roof might just be the most impressive. In front of you, the ground crashes down to Cofete beach, one of the most deserted places of the island. These cliffs are Fuerteventura's botanical treasure trove: they catch the most moisture from clouds and as a result harbour a rich flora, with several endemic species growing here. Look out for Jandía Viper's-bugloss (*Echium handiense*), like the marguerite endemic to the high parts of the peninsula, Fuerteventura Goldcoin (*Asteriscus sericeus*) originally endemic to La Jandía but now planted elsewhere too. The composite Reichardia famarae occurs only here and on the Famara cliffs of Lanzarote and is a relict of times the eastern islands were damper.
To your left and right, the mountain ridge continues, with in the background to the north the sand dunes of the isthmus (site I on page 151) and the rest of the island.

Return the way you came.

Additional sites on Fuerteventura

See map on page 123 for the location of the following sites.

A – Corralejo Natural Park

GPS: 28.699364, -13.841298 The Corralejo Natural Park is an expanse of white sand dunes and a section of Malpaís, complete with a crater that is called the *Montaña Roja* (red mountain). The main road to Corralejo runs straight through the park, and there are various places where you can park. There are no trails in the area, but you can wander to the coast or, inland, into the sand dunes. The main attraction of Corralejo is the Sahara-like landscape of pure-white sand dunes. Along the coast, there are some attractive wildflowers, of which Zygophyllum and Traganum are the most eye-catching. You need to search harder to find the pretty rosettes of the East Canary Sand Crocus* (*Androcymbium psammophillum*), which flowers in late December and January.

The rare East Canary Sand Crocus (*Androcymbium psammophillum*) flowers in sandy barrancos and dune valleys, such as those in the Corralejo Natural Park.

There are some desert birds present as well, but they are hard to find. All in all, Corralejo makes for a wonderful short stop, and is easily combined with a trip to Los Lobos.

B – Malpaís of La Oliva

GPS: 28.628367, -13.917462. About 3.5 km north of La Oliva, a small road, the Calle de los Altos, leads towards a well-developed area of *malpaís*. You can park by the side of the road and walk from there. The rocks are swathed in thick lichen cover; Verode and King Juba's Spurge are the common succulent plants. With some luck you might find Barbary Ground Squirrel, Trumpeter Finch or even a Barbary Partridge, and turning over suitable flat stones could reward you with an Eastern Canary Gecko (often clinging underneath the rock). However, the true reason to visit is one of the larger populations of the rare Caralluma. It perfectly blends in with the rocky malpaís landscape, so search carefully – it is most encountered between rocks on the left side of the trail as indicated on the map.

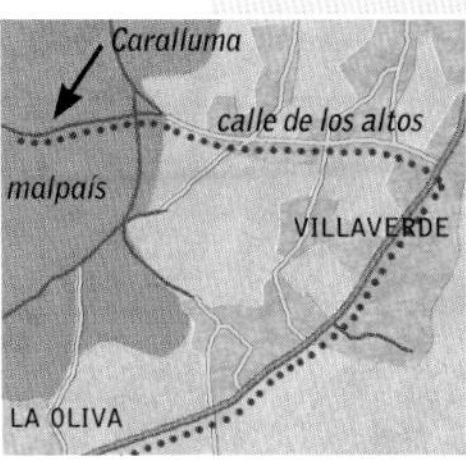

C – 'Ruta de Queso' semi-desert plains

GPS: 28.423705, -13.969663 There is a small but wonderful area of stony desert plain a little east of Antigua in the centre of the island. Although not as good as the main sites in the northwest of Fuerteventura, you may find Houbara, Cream-coloured Courser, Stone Curlew, Trumpeter Finch and Lesser Short-toed Lark here as well.

Coming from the east coast, drive up road from Costa de Antigua towards Triquivijate. Just before the main roundabout in the latter village, take the track to the left, signposted *El Fronton*. Follow it all the way to a barranco, some 4.5 km ahead, while scanning the plains to the left and right of the track.

D – Caleta de Fuste Golf Course

GPS: 28.378173, -13.868891 To exhausted migrant birds, the greens of the Caleta de Fuste Golf course must look from the air like an emerald oasis. The green bushes, fresh grass and (yes!) a freshwater pond attract fatigued migrants like a magnet. In winter, Ruddy Shelducks are common on the greens, navigating between caddies and golf balls.

Take the exit to the golf course and go left at the roundabout to drive along the course. There are plenty of parking facilities and obtaining views over the course is simple. This site is easily combined with a visit to the Salinas and Barranco de la Torre (next two sites).

E – Barranco de la Torre

GPS: 28.356402, -13.878431 Just south of the Salinas de El Carmen, a track leads to the Barranco de la Torre ravine. Some small fields, cliffs, salt marsh, palm trees and thickets of Canary Tamarisk offer a varied landscape in a small area. Several pairs of Egyptian Vulture breed nearby and Plain Swift is common. The Gran Canaria Giant Lizard, up to a metre in length and the largest of the Canary lizards, has been found in this barranco. Although this Gran Canaria endemic was introduced to this small area in Fuerteventura, it is still a wonderful beast to see.

Ruddy Shelducks

You can walk up the Barranco from the coast, which is reached from the track that departs at the Salinas de El Carmen (see map).

The Buzzard is common throughout Fuerteventura, including the Jandía Peninsula. Lizards are its main prey.

F – Cuchillos de Vigan

GPS: 28.324628, -13.898778. The Cuchillos ('knives' in Spanish) of Vigán are a series of parallel, steep mountain ranges, created by erosion of the soft volcanic rock. This is one of the wildest, least inhabited and least visited areas of Fuerteventura, and hence a superb place to explore. The area is important for breeding raptors. The Egyptian Vulture has its highest densities on the island in the Cuchillos and Buzzard, Kestrel and Barn Owl breed as well. There is also a colony of several hundreds of Cory´s Shearwaters (which has one of the weirdest bird calls in the world). During a night visit in the breeding season (April-July) you might hear calling birds. Other Fuerteventura birds as Spectacled Warbler, Trumpeter Finch, Great Grey Shrike, and Stone Curlew also breed. On the pebble beaches, interesting things may wash up, such as the dead Loggerhead Turtle we found here.

The semi-desert plains around Triquivijate (site C), seen from the Betancuria mountains.

The endemic subspecies of Egyptian Vulture (*El Guirre* in Spanish) has its stronghold in the Cuchillos de Vigan.

The only valley with a tarmac road is the one with the small fishermen's village of Pozo Negro at its base – a traditional place that looks like how most villages on Fuerteventura probably did before the tourism sprawl. Of particular interest here is that the three main geological processes that have formed the landscape – eroded valleys, new lava flows and sand – can all be seen in this one valley. In addition, it is one of the places where the Plain Tiger lays its eggs, here on Sodom's Apple Milkweed. The next valley (signposted *Tenicoscuey*) is only serviced by a dirt road to a goat corral, where Egyptian Vultures and Trumpeter Finches often feed.

G – Oasis Park

GPS: 28.187539, -14.157610 The Oasis Park at La Lagita is a popular family excursion. It is a zoo, botanical garden and amusement park all in one. This is not the sort of park you'll usually find in a Crossbill Guide, but in this case, we make an exception because the flowery borders, the palms and many trees (for it really is like an oasis) attract migrant birds, butterflies and dragonflies.

Pulicaria burchardii is a rarity that grows on the Istmo de la Pared near the village of La Pared.

We found Monarch, Canary Red Admiral and Geranium Bronze here, plus Epaulet Skimmer. There is also a small population of Red-vented Bulbuls, which were, inadvertently or deliberately, introduced to the island.
All this can be found on and around the car park – you do not even have to enter the park itself.

H – Istmo de la Pared

GPS: 28.206526, -14.224128 The Isthmus between La Jandía and the rest of Fuerteventura is covered with sand and forms the largest area of dunes on the Canary Islands. Various parts are briefly touched upon in the description of route 12 but can be explored more thoroughly by walking some tracks and trails near the village of La Pared. The beautiful sand landscape, with trails to hidden and little visited beaches, has an interesting flora. The star species are the bindweed *Convolvulus caput-medusae* and the fleabane Pulicaria burchardii (both small dwarf bushes, the first occurs here and in a small area on Gran Canaria; the second only on southern Fuerteventura and the Moroccan coast).
To get here, drive north from Costa Calma and after a little over 2 km, turn left onto a track that leads towards the hamlet of Pueblo del Mar (not signposted). From here, wander around on the trails and tracks. Alternatively, drive into the village of La Pared and continue all the way to the car park on the western end and start exploring from there (GPS: 28.212550, -14.220820).

Oasis Park lives up to its name. The oasis-like environment hosts species like Canary Red Admiral (top). We found an introduced species here, the Red-vented Bulbul (bottom), which appears to be establishing itself at this site.

TOURIST INFORMATION & OBSERVATION TIPS

Travel and accommodation

Travelling to Lanzarote and Fuerteventura

Most visitors arrive by air, as this is the fastest and cheapest. You can grab a flight from many European airports and be on either Fuerteventura or Lanzarote in a few hours. Air fares are variable but generally reasonable although it is usually cheaper to book a package holiday. Such deals exist throughout the year. Since the Canaries are one of closest destinations to Europe where you can enjoy warm winter temperatures, the "cold" season is an important one for tourism. All flights to Lanzarote arrive at Arrecife Airport and flights to Fuerteventura all land at the airport Puerto del Rosario.

The other way is to get to Lanzarote and Fuerteventura by ferry. This brings the added advantage of being able to bring your own vehicle. Regular lines sail once a week from Huelva (26 hours) or Cádiz (36 hours, including a stop at Tenerife) – see **www.navieraarmas.com**.

Travelling on Lanzarote and Fuerteventura

A car is by far the easiest way to travel around Lanzarote and Fuerteventura so, if you want to explore the routes and sites in this guidebook, one is almost indispensable. The roads are generally in very good condition, and even the most distant places are easily accessible from any tourist resort.

Hire cars can be booked in advance at tourist agencies and picked up at the airport. They are not very expensive, but prices on Fuerteventura tend to be somewhat higher than on Lanzarote.

The alternative to the rental car is the public bus service. Buses in Canarian Spanish are called *guaguas* (pronounced *wah-wah*). Though not very fast, the *guaguas* are without doubt the most economical and environmentally friendly way to get from the tourist centres to most of the villages on the islands. The network is extensive – nearly all villages and main junctions are serviced by bus. Services to and from

the airports are offered to various points of the islands. For Fuerteventura, consult **www.tiadhe.com**. Schedules for Lanzarote can be found on **www.arrecifebus.com** and **www.lanzarote.com/es/guaguas**.
Taxis run all over the islands and are cheaper than in most other European countries. Public taxis have a SP license plate (*servicio público*). Consult **www.lanzarotetaxi.com** and **www.taxisfuerteventura.es**.

Accommodation

The offer of hotels and appartments on Lanzarote and Fuerteventura is huge. The best bargains are often package deals (flight plus hotel), and some travel agencies won't sell you anything else. The downside of such deals is that you usually end up in uninspiring tourist flats.
Rural tourism brings you to much more attractive places in more beautiful settings. It is a big step up from the cheap package deals, but also a lot more pricey. To find your accomodation, try **www.airbnb.com** or **www.holiday-rural.com** which offers 32 rural B&B's on Lanzarote and another 12 on Fuerteventura (2013 figures).
It takes almost two hours to drive from Corralejo to Morro Jable – the greatest distance you can travel within a single island. This means that from a central location, all sites are easy to reach. If the desert birds are an important attraction to you, you might want to consider staying close to the dry plains, so that you can make optimal use of the early and late hours of the day. In this case the north of Fuerteventura and the north-central part of Lanzarote are your places of interest.

Shops – opening hours

Shops usually open at 9 am and close at 1 pm, opening again in the afternoon from 3 pm to 7 pm. Large supermarkets don´t close for a lunch-break and stay open later. Banks and post-offices open only in the morning, mostly from 9 am to 2 pm.

Safety issues

Annoyances and hazards

For your own safety, there are two things you need to be careful about on Lanzarote and Fuerteventura: the sunshine and the terrain.
The breeze can be deceivingly cool, so be aware that the solar radiation is very strong. Protect your skin, either by putting on a hat and long-sleeved shirt or by using a high factor (50+) sun cream. Don't forget to take enough water with you to prevent dehydration. Tap water is safe all over the islands, however most is desalinated sea water and doesn't taste very pleasant. Bottled water (*agua mineral*) is widely available, both still (*sin gas*) and carbonated (*con gas*).

When hiking, be aware that many types of lava rocks are rough underfoot. Wear appropriate shoes. It is also advisable to wear some sort of protective water shoes when swimming in rock pools – the underwater lava rocks are just as sharp. In the barrancos, be aware of loose stones and gravel. There are no dangerous or poisonous animals. Crime is not very high on the islands, but to be safe, don't leave your valuables in the car.

Driving on tracks

If you want to reach the more remote places, and especially if you want to see desert birds, you can't avoid driving on unpaved tracks. Some of them are in excellent condition, and easy to drive. Others are not.
The tracks that are most problematic are either too rocky or too sandy. Sandy tracks are tricky because you can easily get stuck in them. Try to avoid them, and if you can't, make sure in advance how long the tricky bit is. If more than 50 metres, turn around. If you do try to cross them, drive in low gear and cross the patch quickly and without stopping. Be careful when driving in barrancos – a perfectly fine track may have one or two difficult spots where water has created a gully. Stay away from steep rocky tracks altogether.
The tracks that are part of car routes described in this book were in good condition at the time of writing – note that even these tracks may have changed due to spells of bad weather or lack of maintenance.
The two main rules of thumb: don't drive a track you don't trust, and make sure you know if your car hire insurance covers driving tracks.

Responsible tourism

The environmentally minded tourist has a difficult time on Lanzarote and Fuerteventura. Apart from the fact that it is hard to visit the islands without using planes and hire cars, finding environmentally sound places to stay is difficult. There are far too many people (both inhabitants and tourists) for the islands to feed or quench the thirst with locally grown products. So most of your food and water is also imported, making the carbon footprint even higher. There is no way of avoiding this (other than not going at all), but you keep your environmental impact lower by being very aware not to waste fresh water and food.
The large number of tourists on such small islands also puts a strain on the wildlife. Here your behaviour does make a difference. Particularly the desert birds are vulnerable to disturbance. Hence be extra careful. Stay in the car to watch them and stay on the roads and tracks. Off road excursions, which are sometimes offered in hotels, are perhaps the most damaging tourism activities on the islands, so don't sign up for one.

Planning your trip

Visiting the other islands

If you have enough time, it is worth visiting one or more of the other Canary Islands. These are quite different in character, having much higher mountains, and being partially covered in a verdant vegetation of laurel forest. A visit to Tenerife is perhaps the most interesting, since it is here that you will find the highest diversity in habitats and species, including many endemics (see Crossbill Guide Tenerife and La Gomera).

You have two options if you want to visit the other Canary Islands: plane or ferry.

Island-hopping by plane: all Canary Islands are interconnected by air by the company Binter Canarias. Most of these flights are daily, or even several times a day. For more information, check **www.bintercanarias.com**.

Taking the ferry: Two companies maintain regular ferry services to other islands: Fred Olson and Naviera Armas. Travelling by boat has the advantage of being less environmentally unfriendly, offering good chances to watch sea birds and dolphins from the boat, and allowing you to bring along your hire car. The downsides are that it is much slower, and that not all islands are connected directly by ferry. A good website to start your search for a ferry connection is **www.directferries.co.uk** and check the destination guide. You can book your tickets directly at the port, or ask your hotel to arrange it for you. Be at least half an hour early and bring your passport with you.

Ferry Crossings

Route	Frequency	Duration
Lanzarote (Playa Blanca) – Fuerteventura (Corralejo)	6 x day	30 minutes
Lazarote (Arracife) – Gran Canaria (Las Palmas)	5 x week	7.5 hours
Lazarote (Arracife) – Tenerife (Santa Cruz)	5 x week	9 hours
Lazarote (Arracife) – La Palma (Santa Cruz)	1 x week	31 hours
Fuerteventura (Puerto Rosario) – Gran Canaria (Las Palmas)	5 x week	7.5 hours / 3 hours
Fuerteventura (Moro Jable) – Gran Canaria (Las Palmas)	5 x week	3 hours / 1.5 hours
Fuerteventura (Puerto Rosario) – Tenerife (Santa Cruz):	5 x week	11.5 hours
Fuerteventura (Moro Jable) – Tenerife (Santa Cruz):	1 x week	6.5 hours

Lanzarote or Fuerteventura?

As each visitor will have a different balance of priorities, it is difficult to give absolute advice as to which island makes the best base. Ideally, try to stay a couple of days on both. If this is not possible, make a day trip to the other islands. Here is a quick comparison guide.

	Lanzarote	Fuerteventura
Scenic beauty	++	+++
Peace and quiet	++	+++
Impressive volcanism	+++	+
Sand dune landscapes	+	++
Flora	++	+
Mammals	-	+
Birdwatching in general	++	+++ (more species)
Steppe birds	++ (easier)	++ (more)
Sea birds (in season)	++	+
migrant waders	++	++
insects	+	+
underwater life	++	+++
walking	++	+

Visiting Fuerteventura from Lanzarote as a day trip

When taking the first boat from Playa Blanco, you can opt for route 8 or 9. Both routes should make it possible for you to see desert birds, including a chance of Trumpeter Finch, Cream-coloured Courser and Black-bellied Sandgrouse, which are hard to find on Lanzarote. Route 9 offers you a good opportunity of seeing the endemic Fuerteventura Stonechat, some waders and wildfowl, including Ruddy Shelduck. The barranco of point 3 of route 8 also offers chances on seeing the chat, plus the Barbary Ground Squirrel.

Visiting Lanzarote from Fuerteventura as a day trip

When taking the first boat from Corralejo, routes 1 and 2 are within easy reach. This offers you the opportunity to visit one of Lanzarote's highlights: the young lava fields and impressive craters of Timanaya National Park. A short stop at the salt works of Janubio (route 2) is additionally of interest for the waders.

When to go

Lanzarote and Fuerteventura are of interest throughout the year, though with some clear seasonal differences.

Breeding birds are mostly sedentary although more active during the breeding period, which is from February to April. The best months for migration are February to March and October to November. By the end of the summer ducks and most waders have left Fuerteventura because reservoirs have dried out. July to October is the better period for sea birds and for breeding Eleonora's Falcons (see box on page 84).

For wildflowers, winter and spring (December to May) are the best although, even in summer, you'll find some flowers in bloom. Winter is the 'rainy season', which means that there are a couple of short spells of rain between long periods of excellent weather. These brief showers do, however, trigger a modest bloom of wildflowers. Reptiles can be found throughout the year, but are less active in winter.
The period between January and May is best for the few dragonflies and butterflies that occur on the islands.

Additional information

Recommended reading

Many, but not all, field guides that cover Europe, also include the Canary Islands. Besides these general guidebooks, we recommend the following books and websites:

Flora It is remarkable that, given the superb flora of the Canary Islands and the large numbers of tourists, there are very few field guides to the flora of the Canary Islands. Bramwell's *Wildflowers of the Canary Islands* (ISBN 847207129) is highly recommended but unfortunately out of print. Hence we also recommend, even to English readers, the German *Kosmos Kanarenflora* (Schönfeld & Schönfelder), which has excellent photographs and information on distribution per island. *Die Farn- und Blütenpflanzen der Kanarischen Inseln*(Muer, Sauerbier & Cabrera Calixto) is a superb book with good desciptions and colour photograps that covers the entire Canary Island flora. It is big though, with over 1300 pages. Joël Lodé (2010): *Succulent Plants of the Canary Islands* is an excellent book with all texts in Spanish, English, German and French. Unfortunately it only covers the succulent plants, which forms only a small portion of the entire flora. Haroun Tabraue, Gil-Rodríguez, Wildpret de la Torre and Prud'Homme van Reine (Author): *Marine Plants of the Canary Islands* is a guide to the sea weeds and sea grasses of the islands. **www.floradecanarias.com**. is a great online resource on the Canarian flora.

Birds and bird finding guides Several field guides go into detail on identification and distribution of Canary Islands birds, e.g. *Field Guide to the Birds of Macaronesia* by Eduardo Garcia del Rey (2011) and *Field Guide to the Birds of the Atlantic Islands* by Tony Clark, Chris Orgill and Tony Disley (2006). Published in 2013 is the *Rare Birds of the Canary Islands* by Eduardo Garcia del Rey and Fransisco Javier García Vargas (order at for example **www.nhbs.com** or **www.lynxeds.com**).

A number of interesting websites on Canarian birds have been launched by fanatic local birdwatchers, some show many excellent photos and others lots of information. Consult **www.birdinglanzarote.blogspot.com.es** and **www.avescanarias.blogspot.com.es**.

Maps Detailed maps of the islands, which include unpaved tracks, can easily be obtained at the airports and bookshops of Lanzarote and Fuerteventura.

Biology and Evolution If you want to understand more about evolution, island ecology and extinctions on islands (including but not exclusively the Canaries), we can recommend two books which read like a novel: David Quammen *The song of the Dodo* and *Demons in Eden* from Jonathan Silvertown. In the Song of the Dodo the author travels all over the world to understand the role of biological isolation and its consequences for nature conservation. Likewise, in Demons in Eden the author travels the globe to understand how it is possible that an evolutionary struggle for the best adaptation leads to a high instead of a low species diversity. In both cases, volcanic islands like the Canaries play a crucial role in understanding these processes.

History The web **mdc.ulpgc.es** with hundreds of photos shows a digital memory of former times.

Observation tips

Hiking on Fuerteventura and Lanzarote

The monotonous landscape of the deserts and lava fields do not make Lanzarote and Fuerteventura hiking paradises. Nonetheless, there are some beautiful walks set out in the area of La Jandía (e.g. route 13) and some others in the mountains of Betancuria (routes 10 and 11). In Lanzarote, most hikes are in the north and they are truly beautiful (see sites J and K on pages 121-122). The beauty of taking walks, other than just the sake of walking itself, is that you will find wildflowers, insects and reptiles more easily. On foot, you'll use all your senses – sound, sight, smell, touch, which is the best way to experience the islands. Note that for safe hiking, you should bring plenty of water and protection against the sun (including sun glasses). The sun and heat can be relentless, and on most trails, there is no shade.

Tracking down desert birds

Searching for birds in the desert takes time and patience as, especially on Fuerteventura, they are thinly spread. Because they are ground nesters, with little defence against predators, most species rely heavily on their camouflage. Therefore, take your time to scan the landscape carefully; it is usually the motion that gives them away. A telescope comes in handy as chances are that the birds are far away. While driving the tracks, keep your windows rolled down, as it is the songs and

calls that tell you there is something around. Goat pens often attract the seed eating birds because of the seed spill from the hay that is fed to the goats.
Even more than in other habitats, birds of deserts are most active at dusk and dawn. At this time, the light is much better too, and there is no heat haze, making it easier to pick out the birds on the ground. Finally, the desert birds are very sensitive, and will press themselves to the ground if someone approaches. Hence it is crucial to stay on tracks and use your car as a hide and drive, very slowly, across the plains.

Tips for sea birdwatching

Lanzarote and Fuerteventura support a large number of sea birds, but they are tricky to see. The best way is by taking a specialised boat trip out to the waters where they frequently feed (see L on page 122). Unfortunately, these trips are very infrequent and relatively costly. Ferry crossings are the next best option. Watching from the coast is the simplest and cheapest option, but birds are likely to be fewer and more distant, making a telescope essential.
There are a couple of good sites for sea birdwatching from land: Tostón (on route 7), La Graciosa (route 6) and Playa Blanca (site B on page 119). The ferries between the islands (see A on page 119) and the ferry to La Graciosa (route 6) are even better. Summer and autumn are the best months (see box on page 84). When going sea watching, consider the following tips:
Timing: The first and last couple of hours of daylight are the best. Both migration (if any) and movement from the nests to the open sea takes place at this time of day. Viewing is also much better as there is no heat haze.
Mild winds are perfect for sea watching. Most seabirds rely on wind to fly, so on completely wind-free days, they tend to stay on the surface. Strong winds are obviously not great as it is hard to keep the telescope steady. However, the hours and days following hard onshore winds can be superb as such winds often push birds closer to land.
Gear: Sea watching without telescope is close to pointless. The more pelagic sea birds (petrels & shearwaters) will be further out over the ocean.
Position: At sea level birds are alternately hidden in wave troughs or visible only as silhouettes against the sky so watch from a vantage point roughly between 10 and 20 metres above sea level. Make sure you have the sun behind you for the best possible light conditions (hence some sites will be 'morning sites' and other ones 'evening sites').

Exploring the underwater world

One of the great ecological treasures of the Canaries lies under water. There is just one problem with the exuberant, colourful submarine world: it is so difficult to explore. Unless you are a skilled scuba diver, you have to make do with a sub-optimal approach. This can still be enormously rewarding, though. Not including professional scuba diving as an option, there are four ways to get to know the marine world.

Snorkelling in sheltered bays: You can snorkel in many places, especially on the east coasts. Look for sheltered bays with a sandy or gravelly beach (easy to get in) and some rocky areas on the side (this is where most of the fish are). Be aware though, that in some seemingly good bays, the current is too strong to swim. If this is the case, authorities will make this known with signs or red flags. Very good places to snorkel are listed as site C on page 119 for Lanzarote, and site A on page 146 for Fuerteventura. The bays between Tarajalejo and Costa Calma on Fuerteventura are also good.

Visiting the Lanzarote Aquarium: This is where you get eye to gill with some of the more spectacular marine animals of the islands. Downside is that it is in a very touristy setting (see page 120).

Taking a trip on a glass bottom boat: Book a seat on a glass bottom boat to La Graciosa (route 6) or to Isla de Lobos off Fuerteventura (site A on page 146; also easy to visit from Lanzarote). On this trip you see the underwater life literally underneath your feet. On the Isla de Lobos you can go snorkelling and enjoy a walk before returning on the glass bottom boat. Check the kiosks alongside the pedestrian zone of the Marina at Corralejo, or **www.fuerteventura.com/lobos/**.

Diving in a submarine: Finally, you can take a submarine catamaran, which allows you to explore the underwater world. Submarine Safaris operates from Puerto Calero on Lanzarote (**www.submarinesafaris.com**; 00 34 928 512898), while Subcat Fuerteventura does so from Morro Jable on Fuerteventura (**www.subcat-fuerteventura.com**; 0034 900 507 006). Both offer complete dives down to about 30 metres to nearby reefs, where you can see mantas, stingrays, sea turtles and barracudas. In both cases there is a diver accompanying the boat, who presents a show with the local wildlife. Although not cheap (prices € 55.- to € 60,- in 2014) and a rather short trip (little more than an hour), this is the closest you get to actually diving in the area.

Birdlist Lanzarote and Fuerteventura

The following bird list includes all breeding and wintering birds plus regular passage migrants. Numbers between the brackets (...) refer to the routes from page 100 onwards. F refers to Fuerteventura and L to Lanzarote.

Grebes Little Grebe is rare (F8). In the 1950's there was a colony at Las Peñitas. Black-necked Grebe is a rare wintering bird in sheltered bays (F, L).

Shearwaters and petrels Cory´s Shearwater is the only sea bird easily seen from the coast and ferry crossings. It is present from March to October (L 6, site A and B on page 119; F7 and 13). (Note that Cory's has recently been 'split' into three near identical species; the nominate form breeds on the islands, the Mediterranean Scopoli's Shearwater is a migrant/winter visitor and the Cape Verde Shearwater a vagrant). Bulwer's Petrel, Barolo Shearwater and – rare – White-faced, European and Madeiran Storm Petrels are seen on ferry crossings (Bulwer's on L6). See also page 84 and 157 for details on sea watching.

Gannets, cormorants and tropicbirds Northern Gannet is rare offshore during winter months. Great Cormorant is seen in increasing numbers. A handful of Red-billed Tropicbirds have been confirmed as breeding on El Hierro, the Chinijo Archipelago and Fuerteventura – they are occasionally seen from vantage points on all sides of both islands, pericularly in the strait between the islands.

Herons, egrets, storks, ibises, spoonbills and flamingos Cattle Egret is farily common near fresh-water and breed (L+F, many on F12). Little Egret and Grey Heron are frequently seen on the coast (e.g. L1 and 6; F8 and 12). Other herons and egrets, storks and Spoonbill are rare but regular vagrants. Small numbers of (feral) Hadada Ibis and Sacred Ibis (both feral) occur on the coast of Jandía, (F12). Greater Flamingos are accidentally found (L1).

Ducks Ruddy Shelduck are now quite common on Fuerteventura (most F8 and site D on page 148). Marbled Teal is fairly rare at Los Molinos (F8). All other ducks are scarce migrants or winter visitors (Most L1 and F8). Almost annually seen are Wigeon, Mallard, Shoveler and Teal, the latter being the commonest winter duck on the islands.

Birds of Prey Buzzard is widespread on Fuerteventura, but rare on Lanzarote (best 4). Egyptian Vulture is locally common on Fuerteventura (best F9, sites F and G on pages 148-149). The situation of the Osprey, Eleonora's and Barbary Falcon is reversed. They are seen mostly at the Famara cliffs (L4 and 6). Common Kestrel is the most abundant breeding raptor on both islands, present in all open areas. Scarce raptors that are reported regularly on passage or in winter include Marsh, Hen and Montagu's Harriers, Sparrowhawk, Black Kite, Booted Eagle, Hobby, Merlin and Peregrine. There is no obvious spot where they consistently occur.

Partridges, rails, crakes and coots Barbary Partridge is a breeding resident on both islands (F 7, 9, 11; on Lanzarote only reliably site F on page 120).
Common Quail is an irregular breeder of fields (L4 and F7). Moorhen and Coot are both residents of Fuerteventura (F8 and site D on page 148).

Bustards The Houbara Bustard is a breeding resident on both islands, more widespread on Fuerteventura (F7, 8 and site D on page 148), but with high densities also on the central plains of Lanzarote (L3).

Waders More than 50 species of waders have been recorded on both islands, the vast majority as vagrants. Regular breeding birds are Black-winged Stilt, Kentish Plover, Little Ringed Plover (e.g. L1 and F8). In winter and on migration Turnstone (common) Ringed Plover (frequent), Whimbrel (frequent), Dunlin (rare), Bar-tailed Godwit (regular), Grey Plover (regular), Redshank (regular) and Greenshank (Regular) occur at the coast (L1 and 6, sites E, H and J on pages 120-121; F7 and 12, sites A, B and E on pages 147-149). Inland wetlands (F8, site I on page 150) and barrancos after rain regularly host wintering Redshank, Greenshank, Common and Green Sandpipers. The sandy coasts (best L1 and F12) often have some Sanderling, Turnstone and Dunlin during the winter.
Breeding residents on the desert plains are Stone Curlew (L3 and 6; F 7, 8, 12 and 13 and site C on page 147) and Cream-coloured Courser (L3 and F 7 and 8; rare at F12 and 13). Both are not uncommon but hard to see.

Skuas, gulls and terns All skua species are present but rare offshore. The Yellow-legged Gull is the only breeding gull and a very common resident. Black-headed Gull and Lesser Black-backed Gull are frequent at the coast in winter in variable numbers. Other gulls are occasional. Sandwich Tern is common during migration periods and winter. Common Tern is a scarce winter visitor and migrant, while Gull-billed Tern is rare during migration periods.

Sandgrouse Black-bellied Sandgrouse is a locally encountered resident in desert habitats on Fuerteventura mostly (best F8). It is the hardest desert bird to find often best located by call as they fly over.

Doves and pigeons Rock Dove is widely distributed on both islands (e.g. L2 and F9). Collared Dove is an abundant resident in built-up areas since it reached the islands in the 1990s. Turtle Dove is one of the few summer visitors e.g. L4). Laughing Dove is a rare resident and breeds on both islands. We found it at Gran Tarajal (F). African Collared Dove is a rare look-alike of Collared Dove. We found it at Haría (L4).

Parakeets Introduced Monk Parakeets maintain a population at Morro Jable (F12). Ring-necked Parakeet breeds in resorts on Lanzarote and is present in various sites on Fuerteventura.

Cuckoos Great Spotted and Common Cuckoo are rare on passage and in winter.

Owls Barn Owl is a rare but widely distributed breeder of cliffs and barns. Long-eared

Owl is scarce and its status as a breeding bird is not clear. Short-eared Owl is a rare winter visitor in open areas.

Swifts Plain and Pallid Swift breed in barrancos and are common from March to October, roughly. Plain Swift is scarce in the winter months. Common Swift is common during migration and winter.

Bee-eaters, Rollers and hoopoes The Hoopoe breeds and is widely distributed in open areas on both islands. Bee-eater and Roller are rare on migration.

Woodpeckers The Wryneck is a rare bird during migration, hiding in trees and shrubs.

Larks Lesser Short-toed Lark (now sometimes called Mediterranean Short-toed Lark) is an abundant resident, breeding in all dry habitats (e.g. L1 and 3 and F 7, 8, 9 and 1). Short-toed Lark is a rare migrant and winter visitor but may be overlooked. Skylark is a rare winter visitor.

Martins and swallows No martins or swallows breed, but Barn Swallow and House Martin are fairly common on passage and rare in winter. Sand Martin and Red-rumped Swallow are scarce migrants.

Pipits and wagtails Berthelot's Pipit is common and widely distributed in open dry habitats. It is probably the most common bird on the islands. Tree Pipit is common on passage during both migration periods. Tawny and Meadow Pipit are scarce on passage and in open fields during winter. Red-throated Pipit is a regular but rare migrant. Recently, Olive-backed Pipit has wintered at Costa Calma (F12). Yellow Wagtail is locally common during migration, especially at irrigated fields and golf resorts (e.g. site D on page 148). Grey Wagtail and White Wagtail are regular but uncommon during migration and in winter.

Thrushes, chats, wheatears, redstarts and allies The Fuerteventura endemic Fuerteventura Stonechat is locally common in gullies and on steep hillsides of the island (e.g. F7, 8, 9, 10, 11 and 13). It is the only species of this group breeding on the islands. Whinchat, Stonechat, Robin and Black Redstart are scarce winter visitors. Nightingale, Bluethroat and Redstart are scarce migrants in resorts. Northern Wheatear is fairly common on migration, while Black-eared Wheatear is a scarce migrant. Song Thrush is a fairly frequent winter visitor.

Warblers Spectacled Warbler and Sardinian Warbler are breeding residents, the first is common in low bushes of dry open areas (L3 and 6, all routes on F) the second is local in lush vegetation and in gardens (L4 and F9, 10, 11 and site F on page 148). Chiffchaff is a common winter visitor to places with tall vegetation. Note that the Canary Chiffchaff is not found on Lanzarote or Fuerteventura, while the status of Iberian Chiffchaff is obscure due to problems of identification. Blackcap (the European race) Willow and Wood Warbler are present in low numbers in tall vegetation. Subalpine Warbler, Whitethroat and Garden Warbler are common migrants, Western Olivaceous Warbler and Melodious Warbler are rare.

Flycatchers Spotted and Pied Flycatcher are scarce migrants, found in gardens and woods. Costa Calma (F12) and Playa Blanca (site B on page 119) are good sites for them.

Tits African Blue Tit is very local in gardens and vegetated areas (L4, F10 and 11).

Shrikes, orioles, bulbuls Great Grey Shrike (subspecies koenigi) is a widespread and common resident in open dry areas of both islands (especially on F). Golden Oriole is a rare migrant, sometimes seen in gardens. The Red-vented Bulbul, introduced from India seems to have established at some resorts on Fuerteventura (site H on page 150).

Crows, starlings and sparrows Raven is a widespread breeding resident of open areas and is easily seen (e.g. L 2 and 4; F9 and 11). The Common Starling is usually a scarce but in some years a common winter visitor. The only sparrow is Spanish Sparrow, which is common in built up areas and resorts.

Finches The Canary is a rare breeding bird of more vegetated areas (L4). On Fuerteventura, Trumpeter Finch is a common resident on the desert plains (e.g. F7, 8, 9, 13). On Lanzarote it is more localised (L1 and site I on page 121). Linnet is a frequent breeding bird of open areas. Greenfinch and Goldfinch have small populations in resorts and other vegetated areas (best L4). Chaffinch, Serin and Siskin are rare winter visitors.

Buntings Corn Bunting is the only resident bunting on the islands, and it is rare (L4 and F7).

PICTURE CREDITS

In the references that follow, the numbers refer to the pages and the letters to the position on the page (t=top, c=centre, b=bottom, with l and r indication left and right).

Aragon Birding / Boyer, David: 31, 108
Aragon Natuurreizen / Woutersen, Kees: 4 (t), 22 (t), 34, 39 (r), 45, 49 (t+b), 60, 61, 68, 72, 101 (b), 107 (t), 115 (b), 128, 131 (t), 133, 149 (b)
Dall'Orto, Giovanni: 75
Crossbill Guides / Hilbers, Dirk: cover, 4 (b), 5 (2nd to 4th from top), 10, 14 (t+b), 19 (r), 20, 24, 25, 26 (t), 27, 30, 33 (t+b), 35, 38, 39 (t+l), 41 (t), 43 (t+b), 47, 50 (t+b), 51 (t), 55, 58 (t+b), 59, 64 (l+r), 66, 67, 69 (t+c), 71, 88, 89 (b), 91, 92 (t+b), 98, 101 (t), 103 (t+b), 104, 105, 110, 111 (b), 112 (t+b), 114, 115 (t), 118, 120, 126 (l+r), 131, 133 (t+b), 134 (lb+rb), 137 (t), 141, 145 (b), 148, 149 (b), 150, (t+b), 151 (t+b)
Crossbill Guides / Swinkels, Constant: 26 (b), 32, 69 (b), 73, 78, 94 (r), 117 (t), 211 (t+b), 125, 126, 134 (b), 136, 140 (t), 145 (t), 146, 152
Grunsven, Roy van: 4 (3rd from top), 36
Janssens, Roelof: 22 (b), 111 (t), 142 (b), 143, 147
Messemaker, Ronald: cover, 4 (2nd from top), 40, 54, 76, 80, 82, 137 (b)
Nijhuis, Nicole van: 5 (top), 84, 122
Raevens, Frederic: image author
Rittner, Oz: 97 (t+b)
Saxifraga / Kruit, Rik: 74 (b)
Saxifraga / Munsterman, Piet: 85 (t+b)
Saxifraga / Skornik, Iztok: 131 (b)
Saxifraga / Vastenhouw, Bart: 117 (b)
SEO-BirdLife / Martin, Aurelio: 46, 81 (l)
Tejera, Gustavo Peña: 74 (t), 81 (r), 89 (t), 107 (b), 148 (t)
Veling, Kars: 93
Versluys, Remco: 19 (l), 41 (b), 51 (b), 62, 90, 96 (t+b), 108 (b), 138, 140 (b)
Verstrael, Theo: 94 (bl)

All illustrations by Crossbill Guides / Horst Wolter

ACKNOWLEDGEMENTS

It is not always easy to compress research, gathering on site information, personal observations and taking photographs in the short period of a field trip. No matter how often you go or long you stay, there are always things you've missed. Hence we are very grateful to everyone who has provided us with photographs, helped us with additional information or verified the drafts we produced. Our special gratitude goes out to Jaap Bouwman, David Boyer of Aragon Birding, Roelof Janssens, Jan-Herman Lamers, Ronald Messemaker, Nicol Nijhuis, Oz Rittner, Jan van der Straaten of Saxifraga Foundation, Gustavo Peña Tejera, Kars Veling and Remco Versluys.

We furthermore thank the team of Crossbill Guides Foundation – not just those who worked on this guidebook and are mentioned in the colophon, but most in particular all those who work behind the scenes to run the organisation or who support the foundation's work financially: Sarah Bakker, Elsbeth Gerritsen, Barbara Kwast, Theo Verstrael, Dennis Wansink, Johanna Winkelman, Louis Wolf and Mart Wolter.

Finally we thank all of Crossbill Guides' partners for their collaboration: Paul Kemmeren, Jack Folkers, Kathrin Ohrmann and all others at KNNV Publishing; Pauline Gosden, Sarah Squibb and Julie McCarron of Vine House, Jan van der Straaten, Marijke Verhagen and all photograpers of Saxifraga Foundation and the people of Swarovski Optik – the latter not only for being a partner of Crossbill Guides but also for their support of the Life project to preserve Houbara Bustards. After all, it is not just about enjoying nature and wildlife – we need to conserve it as well.

Dirk Hilbers and Kees Woutersen
Crossbill Guides Foundation

SPECIES LIST & TRANSLATION

The following list comprises all species mentioned in this guidebook and gives their scientific, German and Dutch names. It is not a complete checklist of the species of North-east Poland. Some names have an asterisk (*) behind them, indicating an unofficial name. See page 7 for more details.

Plants

English	Scientific	German	Dutch
Acacia, Cyclops	*Acacia cyclops*	Rundäuguge Akazie	Roodoogacacia*
Aizoon, Canary	*Aizoon canariense*	Kanaren-Eiskraut	Canarisch ijsplant
Artichoke, Wild	*Cynara cardunculus*	Wilde Artischoke	Kardoen
Asparagus, Pastor's*	*Asparagus pastorianus*	Pastors Spargel	Pastors asperge*
Asphodel, Common	*Asphodelus aestivus*	Kleinfrüchtiger Affodill	Gewone affodil
Asphodel, Thin-leaved*	*Asphodelus tenuifolius*	Dünnblättriger Affodil	Dunbladige affodi
Bassia	*Bassia tomentosa*	Filzige Steppenmelde	Viltig zoutkruid*
Bird's-foot-trefoil, Lanzarote	*Lotus lancerottensis*	Lanzarote-Hornklee	Lanzarote rolklav
Bluebell, Brown	*Dipcadi serotinum*	Schweifblatt	Bruine hyacint*
Boxthorn, Canary	*Lycium intricatum*	Sparriger Bocksdorn	Mediterrane boks
Buttercup, Canary	*Ranunculus cortusifolius*	Kanaren-Hahnenfuss	Canarische boterb
Campylanthus	*Campylanthus salsoloides*	Kanaren-Krummblüte	Canarische kromb
Caralluma, Burchard's	*Caralluma burchardii*	Burchards Fliegenblum	Caralluma
Cistanche, Yellow	*Cistanche phelypaea*	Gelbe Cistanche	Cistanche
Crocus, East Canary Sand*	*Androcymbium psammophillum*	Sandliebendes Androcymbium	Oost-Canarische zandkrokus*
Daisy, Canary Island	*Argyranthemum spec.*	Kanarenmargerite	Canarische margr
Dock, Moon	*Rumex lunaria*	Kanaren-Ampfer	Struikzuring*
Dodder, Alfalfa	*Cuscuta approximata*	Goldgelbe Seide	Gouden warkruid*
Fagonia	*Fagonia cretica*	Fagonie	Fagonia
Fennel, Canary Sea	*Astydamia latifolia*	Nymphendolde	Canarische zeeven
Fennel, Lanzarote Giant*	*Ferula lancerottensis*	Lanzarote-Rutenkraut	Lanzarote-tondervenkel*
Fern, Canary Oak	*Polypodium macaronesium*	Makaronesischer Tüpfelfarn	Canarische eikvar
Fluellen, Thick-leaved*	*Kickxia heterophylla*	Verschiedenblättriges Tännelkraut	Dikbladige leeuwe
Garlic, Rosy	*Allium roseum*	Rosen-Lauch	Roze look
Gold-coin, Fuerteventura*	*Asteriscus sericeus*	Seidenhaariger Goldstern	Fuerteventura dukaatbloem*
Gold-coin, Lanzarote*	*Asteriscus intermedius*	Lanzarote Goldstern*	Lanzarote dukaatbloem*
Gold-coin, Schultz'*	*Asteriscus schultzii*	Schultzes Goldstern	Schultzes dukaatb
Goosefoots	*Chenopodiaceae*	Gänsefusse	Ganzenvoeten
Hare's-ear, Jandia	*Bupleurum handiense*	Jandia-Hasenohr	Jandia-goudscher

iotrope, Shrubby	*Heliotropium erosum*	Ästige Sonnenwende	Struikheliotroop*
ıseleek, Betancuria*	*Aichryson berthencourtianum*	Betancuria-Aichryson*	Betancuria-huislook*
ıseleek, East Canary*	*Aichryson tortuosum*	Ost-Kanaren Aichryson*	Oost-Canarisch huislook*
ıseleek, Lanzarote	*Aeonium lancerottense*	Lanzarote-Aeonium*	Lanzarote-huislook
ıseleek, Sweet	*Aeonium balsamiferum*	Balsam-Aeonium*	Balsem-huislook
Plant, Common	*Mesembryanthemum crystallinum*	Kristall-Mittagsblume	IJsplantje
Plant, Small-leaved*	*Mesembryanthemum nodiflorum*	Knotenblütige-Mittagsblume	Smalbladig ijsplantje*
ga	*Ifloga spicata*	Ährige Ifloga	Aarviltkruid*
naea, Shrubby*	*Launaea arborescens*	Strauch-Dornlattich	Struik doornsla*
rel, Barbusano*	*Apollonias barbujana*	Barbusano	Barbusano laurier*
rel, Bosea	*Bosea yervamora*	Stinkstrauch	Bosea laurier*
rel, Canarian	*Laurus novocanariensis*	Kanaren-Lorbeer	Canarische laurier
ender, Pinnate	*Lavandula pinnata*	Gefiederter Lavendel	Veerbladige lavendel*
dder, Shrubby	*Rubia fruticosa*	Strauchiger Krapp	Struikmeekrap*
llow, Sycamore-leaved*	*Lavatera acerifolia*	Ahornblättrige Strauchpappel	Esdoornbladig kaasjeskruid*
rguarite, Madeira's	*Argyranthemum maderense*	Madeira-Kanaren-margerite	Madeira-margriet*
rguarite, Shrubby	*Argyranthemum frutescens*	Strauchmargerite	Struikmargriet
rguarite, Winter's*	*Argyranthemum winteri*	Fuertenventura-Kanarenmargerite*	Fuerteventura-margriet
nanthes, oose-flowered	*Monanthes laxiflora*	Lockerblütiges Monanthes	Losbloemig vetkruid*
tle, Narrow-leaved*	*Forsskaolea angustifolia*	Schmallblättrige Forsskaolea	Smalbladige netel*
phytum	*Mesembryanthemum theurkauffii*	Theurkauffs Mittagsblume*	Blob-ijskruid*
m, Canary Island Date	*Phoenix canariensis*	Kanarische Dattelpalme	Canarische dadelpalm
ellifolia	*Patellifolia patellaris*	Napffrüchtige Rübe	Komvruchtige biet*
r, Prickly	*Opuntia ficus-indica*	Echter Feigenkaktus	Vijgcactus
nt, One-styled Curry	*Helichrysum monogynum*	Eingriffelige Strohblume	Eenstijllige strobloem*
ycarpaea, Snowy*	*Polycarpaea nivea*	Schneeweisse Vielfrucht	Sneeuwwitte veelvrucht*
chardia, Famara	*Reichardia famarae*	Famara-Reichardie	Famara-reichardia
chardia, Morroccan	*Reichardia tingitana*	Tanger-Reichardie	Marrokaanse reichardia*
tharrow, arrow-leaved	*Ononis angustissima*	Schmallblättrige Hauhechel*	Smalbladig stalkruid*
tharrow, Yellow	*Ononis natrix*	Gelbe Hauhechel	Geel stalkruid
krose, Canary	*Helianthemum canariense*	Kanaren-Sonnenröschen	Canarisch zonneroosje*
krose, Thyme-leaved	*Helianthemum thymiphyllum*	Thymianblättriges Sonnenröschen	Tijmbladig zonneroosje*
stertree	*Calotropis procera*	Oscher	Sodomsappel zijdeplant*
twort, Mediterranean	*Salsola vermiculata*	Wurmförmiges Salzkraut	Mediterraan zoutkruid*
twort, Orotava	*Salsola orotavensis*	Orotava-Salzkraut	Orotava-zoutkruid

Sandwort, Broad-leaved	*Minuartia platyphylla*	Breitblättrige Miere	Breedbladige veldmuur*
Sea-heath	*Frankenia laevis*	Glatte Frankenie	Zeehei*
Sea-lavender, Felty*	*Limonium puberulum*	Flaumhaariger Strandflieder	Viltig lamsoor*
Sea-lavender, Warty*	*Limonium papillatum*	Warziger Strandflieder	Wrattig lamsoor
Sow-thistle, East Canary*	*Sonchus pinnatifidus*	Fiederspaltige Gänsedistel	Veerbladige melk
Spurge, Balsam	*Euphorbia balsamifera*	Balsam-Wolfsmilch	Balsam-wolfsmel
Spurge, Canary	*Euphorbia canariensis*	Kanaren-Wolfsmilch	Canarische wolfsr
Spurge, Jandia	*Euphorbia handiense*	Jandia-Wolfsmilch	Jandia-wolfsmelk
Spurge, King Juba's	*Euphorbia regis-jubae*	König-Juba-Wolfsmilch	Koning Juba wolf
Spurge, Sea	*Euphorbia paralias*	Strand-Wolfsmilch	Zeewolfsmelk
Squill, Broad-leaved	*Scilla latifolia*	Breitblättriger Blaustern	Brede sterhyacint
Stock, Bolle's*	*Matthiola bolleana*	Bolles Levkoje	Bolles violier*
Stonecrop, Naked*	*Sedum nudum*	Nackte Mauerpfeffer*	Naakte muurpepe
Tamarisk, Canary	*Tamarix canariensis*	Kanarische Tamariske	Canarische tamar
Thistle, Willow-leaved Carline	*Carlina salicifolia*	Weidenblättrige Eberwurz	Wilgbladige dried
Tobacco, Tree	*Nicotiana glauca*	Blaugrüner Tabak	Boomtabak
Traganum	*Traganum moquinii*	Moquins Traganum	Traganum
Tree, Casuarina	*Casuarina equisetifolia*	Schachtelhalmblättrige Kasuarine	Casuarina
Tree, Dragon	*Dracaena draco*	Drachenbaum	Drakenbloedboom
Verode	*Kleinia neriifolia*	Oleanderblättrige Kleinie	Kleinia*
Viper's-bugloss, Bonnet's	*Echium bonnetii*	Bonnetts Natternkopf	Bonnets slangenk
Viper's-bugloss, Decaisne's	*Echium decaisnei*	Decaisnes Natternkopf	Decaisne's slangenkruid*
Viper's-bugloss, Jandia	*Echium handiense*	Jandia-Natternkopf*	Jandia slangenkru
Viper's-bugloss, Lanzarote	*Echium pitardii*	Lanzarote Natternkopf	Lanzarote slangenkruid*
Volutaria, Bolle's	*Volutaria bollei*	Bolles Volutarie	Bolles volutaria*
Zygophyllum	*Zygophyllum fontanesii*	Desfontaines-Jochblatt	Zygophyllum*

Mammals

English	**Scientific**	**German**	**Dutch**
Dolphin, Bottlenose	*Tursiops truncatus*	Grosser Tümmler	Tuimelaar
Dolphin, Common	*Delphinus delphis*	Gemeiner Delfin	Gewone dolfijn
Dolphin, Risso´s	*Grampus griseus*	Rundkopfdelfin	Gramper, Grijze d
Dolphin, (Atlantic) Striped	*Stenella coeruleoalba*	Streifendelfin	Gestreepte dolfijn
Hedgehog, Algerian	*Erinaceus algirus*	Wanderigel	Trekegel
Hedgehog, Common	*Erinaceus europeus*	Braunbustigel	Egel
Mouse, House	*Mus musculus*	Hausmaus	Huismuis
Mouse, Lava	*Malpaisomys insularis*	Lava-Maus*	Lava muis*
Pipistrelle, Kuhl's	*Pipistrellus kuhlii*	Weissrandfledermaus	Kuhl's dwergvleer
Rabbit	*Oryctolagus cuniculus*	Wildkaninchen	Konijn
Rat, Black	*Rattus rattus*	Hausratte	Zwarte rat
Rat, Brown	*Rattus norvegicus*	Wanderratte	Bruine rat
Seal, Mediterranean Monk	*Monachus monachus*	Mittelmeer-Mönchsrobbe	Mediterrane monniksrob

ew, Canary	*Crocidura canariensis*	Kanaren-Spitzmaus	Canarische spitsmuis
irrel, Barbary Ground	*Atlantoxerus getulus*	Atlashörnchen	Barbarijse grondeekhoorn
ale, Bryde's	*Balaenoptera brydei*	Brydewal	Brydevinvis
ale, Cuvier´s Beaked	*Ziphius cavirostris*	Cuvier-Schnabelwal	Dolfijn van Cuvier
ale, Fin	*Balaenoptera physalus*	Finnwall	Gewone vinvis
ale, Sei	*Balaenoptera borealis*	Seiwal	Noordse vinvis
ale, Short-finned Pilot	*Globicephala macrorhynchus*	Kurzflossen-Grindwal	Indische griend

rds

glish	Scientific	German	Dutch
cet	*Recurvirostra avosetta*	Säbelschnäbler	Kluut
-eater	*Merops apiaster*	Bienenfresser	Bijeneter
ckcap	*Sylvia atricapilla*	Mönchsgrasmücke	Zwartkop
ethroat	*Luscinia svecica*	Blaukehlchen	Blauwborst
bul, Red-vented	*Pycnonotus cafer*	Russbülbül	Roodbuikbuulbuul
nting, Corn	*Miliaria calandra*	Grauammer	Grauwe gors
tard, Houbara	*Chlamydotis undulata*	Kragentrappe	Westelijke kraagtrap
zard, (Common)	*Buteo buteo*	Mäusebussard	Buizerd
ary	*Serinus canaria*	Kanarengirlitz	Kanarie
ffinch	*Fringilla coelebs*	Buchfink	Vink
ffinch, Blue	*Fringilla teydea*	Teydefink	Blauwe vink
ffchaff	*Phylloscopus collybita*	Zilpzalp	Tjiftjaf
ffchaff, anzarote Island	*Phylloscopus canariensis exsul*	Lanzarote-Zilpzalp	Lanzarote tjiftjaf*
t	*Fulica atra*	Blässhuhn	Meerkoet
morant, Great	*Phalacrocorax carbo*	Kormoran	Aalscholver
rser, Cream-coloured	*Cursorius cursor*	Renvogel	Renvogel
koo, Common	*Cuculus canorus*	Kuckuck	Koekoek
koo, Great Spotted	*Clamator glandarius*	Häherkuckuck	Kuifkoekoek
lew, Stone	*Burhinus oedicnemus*	Triel	Griel
e, African Collared	*Streptopelia roseogrisea*	Lachtaube	Izabeltortel
e, Collared	*Streptopelia decaocto*	Türkentaube	Turkse tortel
e, Laughing	*Spilopelia senegalensis*	Palmtaube	Palmtortel
e, Rock	*Columba livia*	Felsentaube	Rotsduif
e, Turtle	*Streptopelia turtur*	Turteltaube	Tortelduif
lin	*Calidris alpina*	Alpenstrandläufer	Bonte strandloper
le, Booted	*Hieraaetus pennatus*	Zwergadler	Dwergarend
et, Cattle	*Bubulcus ibis*	Kuhreiher	Koereiger
et, Little	*Egretta garzetta*	Seidenreiher	Kleine zilverreiger
con, Barbary	*Falco pelegrinoides*	Wüstenfalke	Barbarijse valk
con, Eleonora's	*Falco eleonorae*	Eleonorenfalke	Eleonora's valk
ch, Trumpeter	*Bucanetes githagineus*	Wüstengimpel	Woestijnvink
mingo, Greater	*Phoenicopterus roseus*	Flamingo	Europese flamingo
catcher, Pied	*Ficedula hypoleuca*	Trauerschnäpper	Bonte vliegenvanger
catcher, Spotted	*Muscicapa striata*	Grauschnäpper	Grauwe vliegenvanger
net, (Northern)	*Morus bassanus*	Basstölpel	Jan van Gent

Godwit, Bar-tailed	*Limosa lapponica*	Pfuhlschnepfe	Rosse grutto
Godwit, Black-tailed	*Limosa limosa*	Uferschnepfe	Grutto
Goldfinch	*Carduelis carduelis*	Distelfink	Putter
Grebe, Black-necked	*Podiceps nigricollis*	Schwarzhalstaucher	Geoorde fuut
Grebe, Little	*Tachybaptus ruficollis*	Zwergtaucher	Dodaars
Greenfinch	*Carduelis chloris*	Grünling	Groenling
Greenshank	*Tringa nebularia*	Grünschenkel	Groenpootruiter
Gull, Black-headed	*Chroicocephalus ridibundus*	Lachmöwe	Kokmeeuw
Gull, Lesser Black-backed	*Larus fuscus*	Heringsmöwe	Kleine mantelmee
Gull, Yellow-legged	*Larus michahellis*	Weisskopfmöwe	Geelpootmeeuw
Harrier, Hen	*Circus cyaneus*	Kornweihe	Blauwe kiekendie
Harrier, Marsh	*Circus aeruginosus*	Rohrweihe	Bruine kiekendief
Harrier, Montagu's	*Circus pygargus*	Wiesenweihe	Grauwe kiekendie
Heron, Grey	*Ardea cinerea*	Graureiher	Blauwe reiger
Hobby	*Falco subbuteo*	Baumfalke	Boomvalk
Hoopoe	*Upupa epops*	Wiedehopf	Hop
Houbara	See: Bustard, Houbara		
Ibis, Hadada	*Bostrychia hagedash*	Hagedasch	Hadada-ibis
Ibis, Sacred	*Threskiornis aethiopicus*	Heiliger Ibis	Heilige ibis
Kestrel, (Common)	*Falco tinnunculus*	Turmfalke	Torenvalk
Kite, Black	*Milvus migrans*	Schwarzmilan	Zwarte wouw
Lark, Lesser Short-toed	*Calandrella rufescens*	Stummellerche	Kleine kortteenleeuwe
Lark, Short-toed	*Calandrella brachydactyla*	Kurzzehenlerche	Kortteenleeuweri
Linnet	*Carduelis cannabina*	Bluthänfling	Kneu
Mallard	*Anas platyrhynchos*	Stockente	Wilde eend
Martin, House	*Delichon urbicum*	Mehlschwalbe	Huiszwaluw
Martin, Sand	*Riparia riparia*	Uferschwalbe	Oeverzwaluw
Merlin	*Falco columbarius*	Merlin	Smelleken
Moorhen	*Gallinula chloropus*	Teichhuhn	Waterhoen
Nightingale	*Luscinia megarhynchos*	Nachtigall	Nachtegaal
Oriole, Golden	*Oriolus oriolus*	Pirol	Wielewaal
Osprey	*Pandion haliaetus*	Fischadler	Visarend
Owl, Barn	*Tyto alba*	Schleiereule	Kerkuil
Owl, Long-eared	*Asio otus*	Waldohreule	Ransuil
Owl, Short-eared	*Asio flammeus*	Sumpfohreule	Velduil
Oystercatcher, Canary Black	*Haematopus meadewaldoi*	Kanarischer Austernfischer	Canarische schole
Parakeet, Monk	*Myiopsitta monachus*	Mönchsittich	Monniksparkiet
Parakeet, Ring-necked	*Psittacula krameri*	Halsbandsittich	Halsbandparkiet
Partridge, Barbary	*Alectoris barbara*	Felsenhuhn	Barbarijse patrijs
Peregrine	*Falco peregrinus*	Wanderfalke	Slechtvalk
Petrel, Bulwer's	*Bulweria bulwerii*	Bulwersturmvogel	Bulwers stormvo
Petrel, Fea's/Zino's	*Pterodroma feae/mollis*	Weichfeder-Sturmvogel	Donsstormvogel
Pipit, Berthelot's	*Anthus berthelotii*	Kanarenpieper	Berthelots pieper
Pipit, Meadow	*Anthus pratensis*	Wiesenpieper	Graspieper
Pipit, Olive-backed	*Anthus hodgsoni*	Waldpieper	Siberische boomp

it, Red-throated	*Anthus cervinus*	Rotkehlpieper	Roodkeelpieper
it, Tawny	*Anthus campestris*	Brachpieper	Duinpieper
it, Tree	*Anthus trivialis*	Baumpieper	Boompieper
ver, Grey	*Pluvialis squatarola*	Kiebitzregenpfeifer	Zilverplevier
ver, Kentish	*Charadrius alexandrinus*	Seeregenpfeifer	Strandplevier
ver, Little Ringed	*Charadrius dubius*	Flussregenpfeifer	Kleine plevier
ver, Ringed	*Charadrius hiaticula*	Sandregenpfeifer	Bontbekplevier
il	*Coturnix coturnix*	Wachtel	Kwartel
en	*Corvus corax*	Kolkrabe	Raaf
shank	Tringa totanus	Rotschenkel	Tureluur
start	*Phoenicurus phoenicurus*	Gartenrotschwanz	Gekraagde roodstaart
start, Black	*Phoenicurus ochruros*	Hausrotschwanz	Zwarte roodstaart
in	*Erithacus rubecula*	Rotkehlchen	Roodborst
ler	*Coracias garrulus*	Blauracke	Scharrelaar
nderling	*Calidris alba*	Sanderling	Drieteenstrandloper
dgrouse, Black-bellied	*Pterocles orientalis*	Sandflughuhn	Zwartbuikzandhoen
dpiper, Common	*Actitis hypoleucos*	Flussuferläufer	Oeverloper
dpiper, Curlew	*Calidris feruginea*	Sichelstrandläufer	Krombekstrandloper
dpiper, Green	*Tringa ochropus*	Waldwasserläufer	Witgat
in	*Serinus serinus*	Girlitz	Europese kanarie
arwater, Cape Verde	*Calonectris edwardsii*	Gelbschnabelsturmtaucher	Kaapverdische pijlstormvogel
arwater, Cory's	*Calonectris borealis*	Gelbschnabelsturmtaucher	Kuhls pijlstormvogel
arwater, Little	See: Shearwater, Macaronesian		
arwater, Macaronesian	*Puffinus baroli*	Makaronesischer Sturmtaucher	Kleine pijlstormvogel
arwater, Manx	*Puffinus puffinus*	Schwarzschnabel-Sturmtaucher	Noordse pijlstormvogel
arwater, Scopoli's	*Calonectris diomedea*	Gelbschnabelsturmtaucher	Scopoli's pijlstormvogel
lduck, Ruddy	*Tadorna ferruginea*	Rostgans	Casarca
veler	*Anas clypeata*	Löffelente	Slobeend
ike, Iberian Grey	*Lanius meridionalis*	Mittelmeer-Raubwürger	Zuidelijke klapekster
kin	*Carduelis spinus*	Erlenzeisig	Sijs
a, South Polar	*Stercorarius maccormicki*	Antarktikskua	Zuidpooljager
lark	*Alauda arvensis*	Feldlerche	Veldleeuwerik
rrow, Spanish	*Passer hispaniolensis*	Weidensperling	Spaanse mus
rrowhawk	*Accipiter nisus*	Sperber	Sperwer
onbill	*Platalea leucorodia*	Löffler	Lepelaar
rling, Common	*Sturnus vulgaris*	Star	Spreeuw
t, Black-winged	*Himantopus himantopus*	Stelzenläufer	Steltkluut
nt, Little	*Calidris minuta*	Zwergstrandläufer	Kleine strandloper
nechat	*Saxicola torquata*	Schwarzkehlchen	Roodborsttapuit
nechat, Canary Island	*Saxicola dacotiae*	Kanarenschmätzer	Canarische roodborsttapuit
nechat, Chinijo	*Saxicola dacotiae murielae*	Chinijo Schmätzer*	Chinijo roodborsttapuit*
rks	*Ciconia spec.*	Storche	Ooievaars
rm-petrel, (European)	*Hydrobates pelagicus*	Sturmschwalbe	Stormvogeltje
rm-petrel, lack-bellied	*Fregetta tropica*	Schwarzbauch-Sturmschwalbe	Zwartbuikstormvogeltje

Storm-petrel, Madeira	*Oceanodroma castro*	Madeirawellenläufer	Madeirastormvog
Storm-petrel, Swinhoe's	*Oceanodroma monorhis*	Swinhoewellenläufer	Chinees stormvog
Storm-petrel, White-faced	*Pelagodroma marina*	Weissgesicht-Sturmschwalbe	Bont stormvogelt
Storm-petrel, Wilson´s	*Oceanites oceanicus*	Buntfuss-Sturmschwalbe	Wilsons stormvog
Swallow, Barn	*Hirundo rustica*	Rauchschwalbe	Boerenzwaluw
Swallow, Red-rumped	*Cecropsis daurica*	Rötelschwalbe	Roodstuitzwaluw
Swift, Common	*Apus apus*	Mauersegler	Gierzwaluw
Swift, Pallid	*Apus pallidus*	Fahlsegler	Vale gierzwaluw
Swift, Plain	*Apus unicolor*	Einfarbsegler	Madeiragierzwalu
Teal	*Anas crecca*	Krickente	Wintertaling
Teal, Marbled	*Marmaronetta anguirostris*	Marmelente	Marmereend
Tern, Common	*Sterna hirundo*	Fluss-Seeschwalbe	Visdief
Tern, Gull-billed	*Gelochelidon nilotica*	Lachseeschwalbe	Lachstern
Tern, Sandwich	*Sterna sandvicensis*	Brandseeschwalbe	Grote stern
Thrush, Song	*Turdus philomelos*	Singdrossel	Zanglijster
Tit, African Blue	*Cyanistes teneriffae deneger*	Östliche Kanarenmeise*	Fuerteventura-pimpelmees
Tropicbird, Red-billed	*Phaethon aethereus*	Rotschnabel-Tropikvogel	Roodsnavelkeerkr vogel
Turnstone	*Arenaria interpres*	Steinwälzer	Steenloper
Vulture, Egyptian	*Neophron percnopterus*	Schmutzgeier	Aasgier
Wagtail, Grey	*Motacilla cinerea*	Gebirgsstelze	Grote gele kwikst
Wagtail, White	*Motacilla alba*	Bachstelze	Witte kwikstaart
Wagtail, Yellow	*Motacilla flava*	Schafstelze	Gele kwikstaart
Warbler, Garden	*Sylvia borin*	Gartengrasmücke	Tuinfluiter
Warbler, Melodious	*Hippolais polyglotta*	Orpheusspötter	Orpheusspotvogel
Warbler, Sardinian	*Sylvia melanocephala*	Samtkopf-Grasmücke	Kleine zwartkop
Warbler, Spectacled	*Sylvia conspicillata*	Brillengrasmücke	Brilgrasmus
Warbler, Subalpine	*Sylvia cantillans*	Weissbart-Grasmücke	Baardgrasmus
Warbler, Western Olivaceous	*Hippolais (pallida) opaca*	Isabellspötter	Westelijke vale spo
Warbler, Willow	*Phylloscopus trochilus*	Fitis	Fitis
Warbler, Wood	*Phylloscopus sibilatrix*	Waldlaubsänger	Fluiter
Wheatear, Black-eared	*Oenanthe hispanica*	Mittelmeer-Steinschmätzer	Blonde tapuit
Wheatear, Northern	*Oenanthe oenanthe*	Steinschmätzer	Tapuit
Whimbrel	*Numenius phaeopus*	Regenbrachvogel	Regenwulp
Whinchat	*Saxicola rubetra*	Braunkehlchen	Paapje
Whitethroat	*Sylvia communis*	Dorngrasmücke	Grasmus
Wigeon	*Anas penelope*	Pfeifente	Smient
Wryneck	*Jynx torquilla*	Wendehals	Draaihals

Reptiles and Amphibians

English	**Scientific**	**German**	**Dutch**
Gecko, Eastern Canary	*Tarentola angustimentalis*	Kanarischer Mauergecko	Oost-Canarische g
Lizard, Atlantic	*Gallotia atlantica*	Ostkanareneidechse	Oost-Canarische h
Lizard, Giant	*Gallotia goliath*	Grosse Rieseneidechse*	Grote reuzenhage

ard, ran Canaria Giant	*Gallotia stehlini*	Gran-Canaria-Rieseneidechse	Gran-Canaria reuzenhagedis
nk, Eastern Canary	*Chalcides simonyi*	Ostkanarenskink	Oost-Canarische skink
tle, Leatherback	*Dermochelys coriacea*	Lederschildkröte	Lederschildpad
tle, Loggerhead	*Caretta caretta*	Unechte Karettschildkröte	Dikkopschildpad

vertebrates

glish	Scientific	German	Dutch
niral, Canary Red	*Vanessa vulcania*	Kanarischer Admiral	Canarische atalanta
niral, Red	*Vanessa atalanta*	Admiral	Atalanta
ck-tip, Greenish	*Euchloe charlonia*	Grünlicher Weissling*	Canarisch marmerwitje
e, African Grass	*Zizeeria knysna*	Amethist- Bläuling*	Amethistblauwtje
e, Common	*Polyommatus icarus*	Hauhechel-Bläuling	Icarusblauwtje
e, Lang's Short-tailed	*Leptotes pirithous*	Kleiner Wander-Bläuling	Klein tijgerblauwtje
e, Long-tailed	*Lampides boeticus*	Grosser Wander-Bläuling	Tijgerblauwtje
etail, Sahara	*Ischnura saharensis*	Sahara-Pechlibelle	Saharalantaarntje
nze, Geranium	*Cacyreus marshalli*	Pelargonien Wanderbläuling	Geraniumblauwtje
wn, Meadow	*Maniola jurtina*	Grosses Ochsenauge	Bruin zandoogje
per, Small	*Lycaena phlaeas*	Kleiner Feuerfalter	Kleine vuurvlinder
ter, Red-veined	*Sympetrum fonscolombii*	Frühe Heidelibelle	Zwervende heidelibel
peror, Blue	*Anax imperator*	Grosse Königslibelle	Grote keizerlibel
peror, Lesser	*Anax parthenope*	Kleine Königslibelle	Zuidelijke keizerlibel
sshopper, urpurarian Stick	*Purpuraria erna*	Ostkanaren-Heuschrecke*	Oostkanarische sprinkhaan*
sshopper, hite-eyed*	Dericorys lobata	Afrikanische Weissaugen-Heuschrecke*	Afrikaanse witoog-sprinkhaan*
nted Lady	*Vanessa cardui*	Distelfalter	Distelvlinder
pet, Fuerteventura	*Patella candei*	Fuerteventura-Napfschnecke	Fuerteventura schaalhoren*
ster, Jameos Blind	*Munidopsis polymorpha*	Jameos Albinokrebs*	Jameos blinde kreeft*
ust, Egyptian	*Anacridium aegyptium*	Ägyptische Wanderheuschrecke	Egyptische treksprinkhaan
ntis, etancourt's Praying*	*Pseudoyersinia betancuriae*	Betancourt's Gottesanbeterin*	Betancourt's bidsprinkhaan*
rant, African	*Catopsilia florella*	Afrikanischer Einwanderer	Gele trekvlinder
narch	*Danaus plexippus*	Monarchfalter	Monarchvlinder
rlet, Broad	*Crocothemis erythraea*	Feuerlibelle	Vuurlibel
mmer, Epaulet	*Orthetrum chrysostigma*	Rahmstreif-Blaupfeil	Epauletoeverlibel
er, Plain	*Danaus chrysippus*	Afrikanischer Monarch	Kleine monarchvlinder
ite, Bath	*Pontia daplidice*	Reseda Falter	Resedawitje
te, Fuerteventura reen-striped	*Euchloe belemia*	Grüngestreifter Weissling	Gestreept marmerwitje
ite, Large	*Pieris brassicae*	Grosser Kohlweissling	Groot koolwitje
ite, Small	*Pieris rapae*	Kleiner Kohlweissling	Klein koolwitje
ow, Clouded	*Colias crocea*	Postillion	Oranje luzernevlinder